rebuilding

when your relationship ends

bruce fisher

Impact Publishers
POST OFFICE BOX 1094
SAN LUIS OBISPO, CALIFORNIA 93406

Fifth Printing, March, 1983

Copyright © 1981
Bruce Fisher

PUBLISHER'S NOTE

This publication is designed to provide accurate and authoritative information in regard to the subject matter covered. It is sold with the understanding that the publisher is not engaged in rendering psychological, medical, or other professional services. If expert assistance or counseling is needed, the services of a competent professional should be sought.

Library of Congress Cataloging in Publication Data

Fisher, Bruce, 1931-
  Rebuilding : when your relationship ends.

  Bibliography: p.
  1. Divorce. Psychological aspects. 2. Interpersonal relations. I. Title.
  HQ814.F53   301.42'84   79-24440
  ISBN 0-915166-30-5

Cover design and illustrations by Sharon Schnare

Printed in the United States of America

Published by
Impact 〰 Publishers
POST OFFICE BOX 1094
SAN LUIS OBISPO, CALIFORNIA 93406

DEDICATION

This book is dedicated to...

...the thousands of people that, while I was attempting to teach them in the Divorce and Personal Growth Seminars, taught me much of what is in this book.

...my children Todd and Sheila who, with their profound comments about life, teach me a great deal.

...my parents Bill and Vera because the more I understand life, families, and myself, the more I appreciate the gift of life they gave me.

...and my late wife Carol, who continually taught me with her love what it means to be a man and a human being.

AND A WORD OF THANKS

...to my editor and publisher, Bob Alberti, who helped it turn out the way I wanted it to.

Bruce Fisher, Ed.D.
Family Relations Learning Center
450 Ord Drive
Boulder, Colorado 80303

table of contents

foreword

Virginia M. Satir

Divorce is a metaphorical surgery which affects all areas of life of the individual. I have often said that the roots of divorce are in the circumstances and hopes at the time of marriage. Many, many, many people marry with the idea that life is going to be better. Perhaps only a fool would enter into marriage thinking that would not be the case. The depth of disappointment at the time of divorce will depend upon how much more one wants to get out of life or how much more one feels it necessary to add someone to one's life to make life worthwhile.

For many people, divorce is a broken experience, and before they can go on with their lives, they need to be able to pick up the pieces. This period often includes deep emotional feelings of despair, disappointment, revenge, retaliation, hopelessness and helplessness. They need to develop a whole new orientation to the life that will come. And they need time to mourn what was hoped and to realize that the hope will not manifest itself.

Many books on divorce talk only about the problems. Of course, there are the injury to the ego, diminished feeling of self-worth, constant nagging questions about what went wrong, and many fears about the future. Dr. Fisher has given a very practical and useful framework within which to examine the brief period, to take a look at where one is, and to point directions for the future. He offers step-by-step guides to getting oneself in a position to enjoy the life that comes after the divorce. He presents it as a period in which one can learn from the past, get to know oneself better, and also to help to develop new parts of the self that were previously unknown. An apt analogy would be that of a convalescence which occurs after any kind of surgery.

1

2

The emotional levels one needs to work through during and following divorce are very much parallel to the stages one goes through at the time of death. At first, there is a denial of the events that have taken place and a consequent feeling of wanting to isolate oneself from the whole situation. Then anger, wherein one blames someone else for one's predicament. The third level is bargaining; a kind of situation in which one wants to look at the ledger to see that things are equal. This is often manifest over the custody of children and property settlements at the time of divorce. Then comes a period of depression, which is where much self-hatred, self-blame and feelings of failure are present. Finally, after all of this, one comes to the acceptance of the situation and an acceptance of the self. Out of this comes hope for what can happen.

I believe Bruce Fisher's book makes it possible for people to work through these various levels, stage-by-stage. It is important to give this "rebuilding" period the time it needs, to awaken parts of the self that have been paralyzed, repressed, or unknown. Let each self — in this case the divorced person — come into the next part of life with hope rather than failure!

Menlo Park, California
September 1980

The REBUILDING BLOCKS

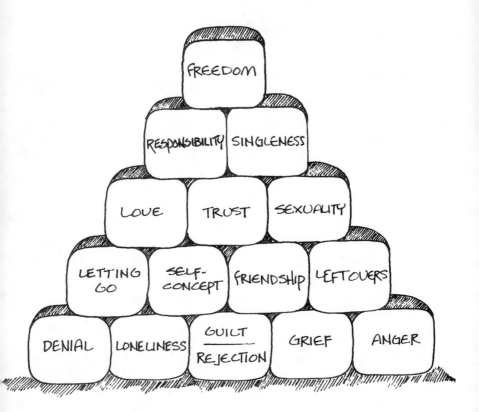

You are probably experiencing the painful feelings that come when a love-relationship ends. There is a proven 15-step process of adjustment to the loss of a love. This chapter provides an overview and introduction to the Rebuilding Blocks which form that process.

chapter one

Are you hurting? If you have recently ended a love-relationship, you are. While some people *appear* not to hurt when their love-relationships end, I believe they have either already worked through a lot of hurt, or else they have yet to feel the pain.

So go ahead, acknowledge that you are hurt. It is natural, expected, healthy, even *okay* to hurt. Pain is nature's way of telling us that something in us needs to be healed, so let us get on with the healing.

Can I help? Well, I can share with you some of the learning that takes place in the seminars that I have been conducting for several years. The growth that takes place in people during a 10-week seminar is remarkable. Maybe by sharing some of these ideas with you, I can help you learn how to get through the hurt also.

There is an adjustment *process* — with a beginning, an end, and specific steps of learning along the way. While you are feeling some of the pain, you are more anxious to learn how to be healed. You, like most of us, probably have had some destructive patterns of behavior for years — maybe since your childhood. While you were in the love-relationship, it was difficult to change, and you might have been comfortable enough that you felt no need to change. But now there is that pain. What do you do? Well, you can use the pain as motivation to learn and to grow. It is not easy. It takes a lot of hard work.

I have arranged the steps of the adjustment process into a pyramid of *Rebuilding Blocks* to symbolize a mountain. Rebuilding means climbing that mountain, for most of us a difficult journey. Some people do not have the strength and stamina to make this difficult journey, and stop off somewhere on the trail. Some of us become seduced into another important love-relationship before learning all that we can from the pain. All these drop out before reaching the top, and they miss the magnificent view of life that comes from climbing the mountain. (You can probably guess that I live in Colorado near the mountains!) Some of us withdraw into the shelter of a cave in our own little world and watch the procession go by — we never reach the top either. And, sadly, there are a few who choose self-destruction, jumping off the first cliff that looms along the trail.

Let me assure you that the climb is worth it! The rewards at the top make the tough climb worthwhile.

How long will it take to climb the mountain? My studies with the *Fisher Divorce Adjustment Scale.*[1] indicate that on the average it takes about a year to get up above the tree line (past the really painful, negative stages of the climb), longer to reach the top. Some will make it in less time, others in more. Some research suggests that a few in our climbing party will need as long as three to five years. But do not let that discourage you. *Finishing* the climb is what counts, not how long it takes. Just remember that you climb at your own rate, and do not get rattled if some pass you along the way. Like life itself, the *process* of climbing and growing is the source of your greatest benefits!

I have learned a great deal about what you are going through by listening to the people in my seminars. People sometimes interrupt one of my talks and ask, "Were you *eavesdropping* when my ex and I were talking last week? How did you know what he (she) was saying?" Well, although each of us is an individual, with unique experiences, there are similar patterns that all of us go through while ending a love-relationship. When I talk about patterns, you will likely find it will be more or less the pattern you are experiencing.

These patterns are similar not only for the ending of a love-relationship, but for any *ending* crisis that comes along in your life. Frank, a participant in one of my seminars, reports that he followed the same patterns when he left the priesthood of the Catholic Church. Nancy found the same patterns when she was fired from her job, Betty when she was widowed. Maybe one of the most important personal skills we can develop is how to adjust to a crisis. Probably there will be more crises in our lives, and learning to shorten the pain time will be a highly valuable learning experience!

In this chapter I will briefly describe the trail that we will be taking up the mountain. In the following chapters we will get on with the emotional learning of actually climbing the mountain. I suggest that you start keeping a journal right now to make the climb more meaningful. After the journey is over, you can re-read your journal to gain a better perspective on your changes and growth during the climb. More about journals at the end of this chapter.

The rebuilding blocks model graphically shows 15 specific feelings and attitudes, arranged in the form of a pyramid to symbolize the mountain that must be climbed. Indeed, the adjustment can be as difficult a journey as climbing a mountain. At first the task is overwhelming. Where to start? How do I climb? How about a guide and a map to help us climb this difficult mountain? That is what the rebuilding blocks are — a guide and a map prepared by others who have already traveled the trail. As we climb, we'll discover that tremendous personal growth is possible, despite the emotional trauma we experienced from ending a love-relationship.

Throughout the book you will find specific ways of dealing with each rebuilding block to prevent it from becoming a stumbling block. (You have probably already stumbled enough!) People often report that they can immediately identify their blocks which need work. Others are unable to identify a problem block because they have effectively buried their feelings and attitudes about it. As a result, at some higher point on the climb, they may discover and explore the rebuilding blocks overlooked at first. Cathy, a volunteer helper in one of my seminars, suddenly recognized one during an evening class: "I've been stuck on the Rejection rebuilding block all along without realizing it!" The following week she reported considerable progress, thanks to identifying the problem!

On the following pages is a pre-journey briefing on the climb.

I. *DENIAL* : "It'll Never Happen to Me"

None of us plans to be divorced. In our marriage vows, we promised commitment "till death us do part." Divorce only happened to others, but would never happen to us!

But divorce does happen for some of us. We discover that our love-relationship is ending, but we don't want anyone to know. We are afraid to admit failure, and we fear rejection by our friends. Throughout our lives, from the news media, church sermons, and teachers at school, we have been taught that divorce is wrong and destructive. It may feel as though a big "D" (for *Divorced*) suddenly appears on one's forehead. We want to deny that divorce is part of *our* lives.

Nona talked hesitantly about taking the 10-week seminar, and finally was able to describe her hesitation. "If I took the divorce seminar, it would mean that my marriage is over, and I don't want to accept that yet."

II. From *LONELINESS* to Aloneness

When a love-relationship ends, the feeling is probably the greatest loneliness one has ever known. Many daily living habits must be altered now that the other person is gone. The couple may have spent time apart before, but the partner was still in the relationship, though not physically present. When the *relationship* is ending, the partner is not there. Suddenly you are totally alone.

The thought, "I'm going to be lonely like this forever," is overwhelming. It seems we are never going to know the companionship of a love-relationship again. We may have children living with us and friends and relatives close to us, but the loneliness is somehow greater than all of the warm feelings these loved ones have for us. Will this empty feeling ever go away? Can I ever feel okay about being alone?

III. *REJECTION vs. GUILT: Dumpers 1, Dumpees 0*

Have you heard the terms *dumper* and *dumpee* before? No one who has experienced the ending of a love-relationship needs definitions for these words. Usually there is one person who is more responsible for deciding to end the love-relationship; that person becomes the dumper. The more reluctant partner is the dumpee. Most dumpers feel guilty for hurting the former loved one. Dumpees find it tough to acknowledge being rejected.

The adjustment process is different for the dumper and the dumpee, since the dumper's behavior is largely governed by feelings of guilt, and the dumpee's by rejection. Until our seminar discussion of this topic, Dick had maintained that his relationship ended mutually. He went home thinking about it, and finally admitted to himself that he was a dumpee. At first, he became really angry! Then he began to acknowledge his feelings of rejection, and recognized that he must deal with them before he could continue the climb.

IV. *GRIEF:*   Big Boys — and Girls — Do Cry

Grief is an important part of the recovery process. Whenever we suffer the loss of love, the death of a relationship, the death of a loved one, or the loss of a home, we must grieve that loss. Indeed, the divorce process has been described by some as largely a grief process. Grief combines overwhelming sadness with a feeling of despair. It drains us of energy by leading us to believe we are helpless, powerless to change our lives. Grief is a crucial rebuilding block!

One of the symptoms of grief is a loss of body weight, although a few people do gain during periods of grief. I was not surprised when I overheard Glenda telling Harriet, "I need to lose weight — guess I'll end another love-relationship!"

V. *ANGER:* Damn the S.O.B.!

It is difficult to understand the intensity of the anger felt unless one has been through divorce. When I lecture, I frequently tell a true story that appeared in the *Des Moines Register* a few years ago. It helps me to find out if the audience is primarily composed of divorced or married people: While driving by the park, a female dumpee saw her male dumper lying on a blanket with a girl friend. She drove into the park and ran over the former spouse and his girl friend with her car! Divorced people respond by exclaiming, "Right on! Did she back over them again?" Married people, not understanding the divorce anger, will gasp, "Ugh! How terrible!"

Most divorced people were not aware that they would be capable of such rage because they had never been this angry before. This special kind of rage is specifically aimed toward the ex-love-partner; and it can be really helpful to your recovery, since it helps you gain some needed emotional distance from your ex.

VI. *LETTING GO* of the Emotional Corpse

It is tough to let go of the strong emotional ties which remain from the dissolved love-union. Nevertheless, we must stop investing emotionally in the dead relationship.

Stella, whom you'll meet again in chapter seven, came to take the seminar about four years after her separation and divorce; she was still wearing her wedding ring! To invest in a dead relationship, an emotional corpse, is to make an investment with no chance of return. The need instead is to begin investing in productive personal growth, which will help in working one's way through the divorce process.

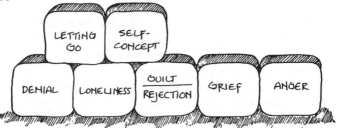

VII. *SELF-CONCEPT:* Maybe I'm Not So Worthless After All!

Feelings of self-worth and self-esteem greatly influence behavior. Low self-esteem and a search for stronger identity are major causes of divorce; divorce, in turn, causes lowered self-esteem and loss of identity. For many people, self-concept is lowest when they end the love-relationship. They have invested so much of themselves in the love-relationship that when it ends, their feelings of self-worth and self-esteem are devastated.

"I feel so worthless that I can't even get out of bed in the morning," reports Jane, "and if I do get out of bed, I am unable to make my bed. I go all day thinking about that unmade bed, and make so many typing mistakes at work that I'm probably going to be fired." Such a preoccupation with trivia commonly accompanies low self-esteem.

Rebuilding one's self-concept is a tough job, and, as we will consider in detail in chapter eight, requires much time and energy.

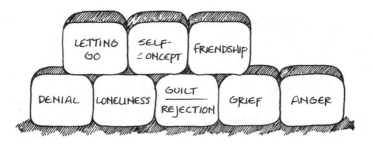

VIII. *FRIENDSHIPS:* Where Has Everybody Gone?

The seven rebuilding blocks that tend to be the most painful usually occur early in the process. Because they are so painful, there is a great need for friends to help one face and overcome the emotional pain. Unfortunately, many friends are usually lost as one goes through the divorce process, a problem that is especially evident for those who have already physically separated from the love-partner. The problem is made worse by withdrawal from social contacts because of emotional pain and fear of rejection. Divorce is threatening to friends, causing them to feel uncomfortable around the dividing partners.

Betty says that the old gang of couples had a party this weekend, but she and her ex were not invited. "I was so hurt and angry. What did they think — that I was going to seduce one of the husbands or something?" Social relationships may need to be rebuilt around friends who will understand our emotional pain without rejecting us. It is worthwhile to work at retaining some old friends, and finding new friends to support and listen.

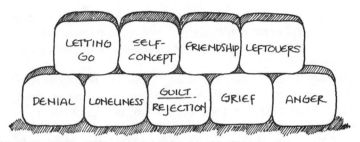

IX. *LEFTOVERS:* They're Not All in the Refrigerator!

Leftovers comprise all the difficulties which remain from your past and your previous love-relationship. You thought you had left these behind; but when you begin another relationship, you find the leftovers are still there (or, as Ken said to me, "Those damn neuroses follow me everywhere!").

The person who has a need to bring home "stray cats" to nurture back to good health often ends up *marrying* one of these cats. This person will continue to bring home stray cats until he/she makes some basic personality changes. I asked one woman how she would feel if she discovered she had taken home another stray cat the next time she got married. The big male policeman in the class interrupted to ask, "How do you think it feels to *be* a stray cat?"

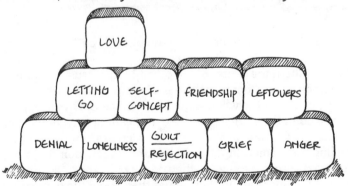

X. *LOVE* Thyself As Thy Neighbor

The typical divorced person says, "I thought I knew what love was, but I guess I was wrong." Ending a love-relationship should encourage one to re-examine what love is. A feeling of *unloveable-ness* may be present at this stage. "Not only do I feel unloveable now, but I'm afraid I never *will* be loveable!" This fear can be overwhelming.

Long ago I heard a sermon titled, "Love Thy Neighbor As Thyself," which asked, "What happens if you don't love yourself?" Many of us place the center of our love in another person rather than in ourselves. When divorce comes, the center of our love is removed, adding to the trauma of loss. An important element in the rebuilding process is to learn to love ourselves. If we do not love ourselves, how can we expect anybody else to love us?

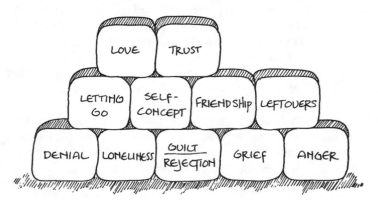

XI. *TRUST:* Foundation for Healthy Relationships

Located right in the center of the pyramid, the trust rebuilding block symbolizes the fact that the basic level of trust, within yourself, is the center of the whole adjustment process. Divorced people frequently point their fingers and say they cannot trust anyone of the opposite sex. There is an old cliche which fits here: when you point a finger at something, there are three fingers pointing back at you. When divorced people say they do not trust the opposite sex, they are saying more about themselves than about the opposite sex!

The typical divorced person has a painful love-wound resulting from the ending of the love-relationship, a love-wound which prevents him/her from loving another. It takes a good deal of time to be able to risk being hurt and to become emotionally close again.

Incidentally, keeping that distance can be hazardous, too! Lois says that when she returned home from her first date, there was a mark on the side of her body caused by the door handle on the car — she was attempting to get as far away from him as possible!

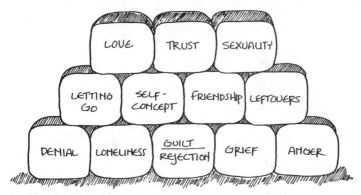

XII. *SEXUALITY:* It's Beautiful!

What do you think of when the word *sex* is mentioned? Most of us tend to react emotionally and irrationally. Our society overemphasizes and glamorizes sex. Married couples often imagine divorced people as oversexed and free to "romp and play in the meadows of sexuality" the whole night long. In reality, single people often find the hassles of sexuality among the most trying in the divorce process.

A sexual partner was available in the love-relationship. Even though the partner is gone, sexual needs go on. In fact, at some points in the divorce process, the drive is greater than before.

Most people are more or less terrified by the thought of dating — feeling like teenagers again — especially when they sense that somebody has changed the rules since they dated earlier. They feel old, unattractive, unsure of themselves, and fearful of awkwardness. And to top it off, they have the "parent morality" that tells them to be "good little boys and girls." Not only are their *parents* telling them what they should do, their own *teenagers* may delight in *parenting* them! ("Be sure to get home early, Mom.") Thus, for many, dating is confusing and uncertain. No wonder sexual hang-ups are so common!

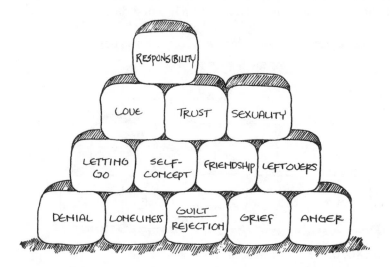

XIII. *RESPONSIBILITY*: Let's Treat Each Other As Adults

"What can we learn from the crisis of an ended love? How can we improve our future relationships?" Such vital questions bring us to the issue of equal responsibility relationships. Almost 100 percent of the people participating in my divorce and personal growth seminars admit that their marriages were largely over- and under-responsible relationships. Somebody was *taking care of* somebody. People in parent-child relationships are not able to adjust to stress and changes within themselves and in the relationships. Partners find it easier to grow and to be themselves when they relate on an adult level. It takes time and effort to learn how to build relationships. Chapter fourteen offers some valuable tips.

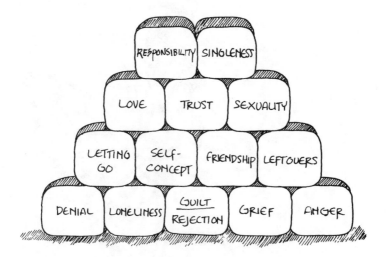

XIV. *SINGLENESS:* You Mean It's Okay?

People who went directly from their parental homes into "marriage homes" without having a period of singleness often missed this important growth period entirely. Even college may have been supervised by "parental" figures and rules.

Regardless of your previous experience, however, a period of singleness — growth as an independent person — will be valuable *now.* Such an adjustment to the ending of a love relationship will allow you to really let go of the past, to learn to be whole and complete within yourself, and to invest in yourself. Singleness is not only *okay,* it is *necessary!*

Joan came up to me in a seminar after I had discussed singleness. She was elated and said, "I'm enjoying being single so much that I felt I must be abnormal. You make me feel normal being happy as a single person. Thanks!"

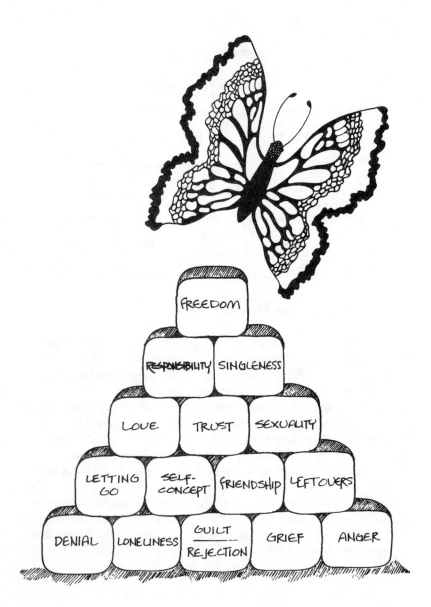

XV. *FREEDOM:* From Chrysalis to Butterfly

The final stage has two dimensions. The first is freedom of *choice.* When you have worked through all of the rebuilding blocks that have been stumbling blocks in the past, you are free to enter into another relationship. You can make it more productive and meaningful than your past love-relationship. You are free to choose happiness as a single person or in another love-relationship.

There is another dimension of freedom: the freedom to *be yourself.* Many of us carry around a burden of unmet needs, controlling us and not allowing us freedom to be the persons that we want to be. As we unload this burden and learn to meet needs that were formerly not met, we become free to be ourselves. This may be the most important freedom.

We have now looked at the process of adjustment as it relates to ending a love-relationship. While climbing the mountain, one occasionally slips back to a rebuilding block which may have been dealt with before. I listed the blocks from one to fifteen, but they are not necessarily dealt with in that order. In fact, one is more or less working on all of them together. And another big setback, such as court litigation or the ending of another love-relationship, may result in a backward slide some distance down the mountain.

Some people ask how religion relates to the rebuilding blocks. Many people working through divorce find it difficult to continue their affiliation with the church they attended while married for several reasons. Many churches still look upon divorce as a sin. Many people continue to feel guilt within themselves whether the church condemns them or not. Churches frequently are very family oriented. Single parents and children of divorced people may be made to feel different, not belonging in church. Many people become distant from the church since they are unable to find comfort and understanding as they are going through the divorce process. This distance leaves them with more loneliness and rejection.

Happily, many churches are beginning to be concerned about meeting the needs of people working through the divorce process, a helpful attitude. I encourage my class participants to inform the church of their needs by developing a singles group, by talking to an

adult Sunday School class, and by sharing with the minister their
feelings of rejection and loneliness perhaps fostered by members of
the church. You may wish to aproach your church to inform others of
the needs of people who are ending their love-relationships.

My personal belief is that the rebuilding block concept is what religion is all about. I believe that the way we live reflects religious
faith, and that God wants us to develop and grow to our fullest potential. Thus, learning to adjust to a crisis is a spiritual process as
well. The quality of relationships we build with the people around
us, and the amount of love, concern, and caring that we are able to
show in these relationships are good indications of our relationship
with God.

"What about the **children**?" Many people ask about kids and how
the rebuilding blocks relate to them. The process of adjustment for
kids is very similar to that for adults. The rebuilding blocks apply to
the children (as they may to other relatives such as grandparents,
aunts, uncles and close friends). Many parents get so involved in
trying to help their *kids* work through the adjustment process that
the parents neglect to meet their own needs. If you are a parent who
is embarking on the Rebuilding journey, my suggestion is that you
learn to take care of yourself and the adjustment process that *you*
need. You will find that your children will tend to adjust more easily
as a result. The nicest thing you can do for your kids is to get *your*
act together. Kids tend to get hung up in the same rebuilding blocks
as their parents, so by making progress for yourself, you will be
helping your children too. In our discussion of each rebuilding block
in the chapters to come, we will take up the implications of that
stage for the kids.

Many people are reading self-help books these days, learning the
vocabulary and gaining an intellectual awareness, but not learning
emotionally from the experience. *Emotional learning* includes those
experiences which register in your *feelings*, such as: mothers are
usually comforting; certain kinds of behavior will bring punishment;
ending a love-relationship is painful. What we learn emotionally affects our behavior a great deal, and much of the learning we have to

do to adjust to a crisis is emotional *relearning*. The things we believed all of our lives may not be true and we have to relearn. The intellectual learning is of little value until we learn emotionally.

Because emotional learning is so important, I have included in this book exercises to help you relearn emotionally. Many chapters have some specific exercises for you to do before reading the next chapter in the book.

Here are your first homework exercises:

1. Keep a journal or a diary in which you write down your feelings. You might do it daily, weekly, or whenever it fits your schedule. Start a lot of the sentences in the journal with "I feel — " because that should help you write more feelings. Writing a journal will not only be an emotional learning experience that will enhance your personal growth, but it will also provide a yardstick to measure your personal growth. People often come back months later to read what they wrote and are amazed at the changes they have been able to accomplish. I cannot remember anyone who has written a journal who has not found it to be a worthwhile experience. I suggest you start writing the journal as soon as you finish reading this chapter. You may want to write in your journal after reading each chapter of the book.

2. The rebuilding block model usually enables people to identify the stumbling blocks in their own divorce process. Think about each of the 15 rebuilding blocks and determine which blocks you need to consider in depth in your own life.

3. Because a support system is so important, another part of the homework concerns building a support group. I suggest you find one or more friends, preferably of both sexes, and discuss the rebuilding blocks with which you are having difficulty. This sharing may be easier for you with a person who has gone or is going through the divorce process himself/herself, because many married people may have difficulty relating to your present feelings and attitudes. Most important, however, is your *trust* in that person.

If you choose to form a discussion group of supportive friends, you may find this book a helpful guide as each of you progresses up the mountain.

Learn to ask another person for help. Call someone whom you feel you would like to get to know better and start building a friendship.

Use any reason you need in order to get started. Tell the person
about this homework assignment if you like. You are learning to
build a support system of friends. Reach when you are feeling
somewhat secure, so that when you are down in the pits (and it is
tough to reach out when you are down there!), you will be able to
reach out to at least one friend who can throw you an emotional life-
line.

4. At the end of each chapter you will find a series of statements
— most of them adapted from my *Fisher Divorce Adjustment Scale*
— which I have included as a check list for you. I suggest you take
the time to answer them, and let your responses help you decide
how ready you are to proceed to the next rebuilding block. (If you
would like to take the complete *Fisher Divorce Adjustment Scale*,
contact a professional counselor or psychologist, who can
administer, score, and interpret the *Scale* for you. For more information about the *FDAS*, see page 199.

Here is the first set of check list statements for you to respond
to before you start reading the next chapter. You may wish to
assess your response to each question as *satisfactory, I need to
improve,* or *unsatisfactory.*

1. *I have identified the rebuilding blocks that I need to work on.*
2. *I understand the adjustment process.*
3. *I want to begin working through the adjustment process.*
4. *I want to use the pain of this crisis to learn about myself.*
5. *I want to use the pain of this crisis as motivation to experience
   personal growth.*
6. *If I am reluctant to grow, I will try to understand what feelings
   are keeping me from growing.*
7. *I will keep my thoughts and feelings open to discover any rebuilding blocks that I may be stuck in at the present time.*
8. *I have hope and faith that I can rebuild from this crisis and
   make it into a creative learning experience.*
9. *I have discussed the rebuilding blocks model of adjustment
   with friends in order to better understand where I am in the
   process.*

DENIAL: It'll Never Happen to Me!

Ending a love-relationship may be the greatest emotional pain you will ever experience. The pain is so great, in fact, you may react with denial or disbelief. This only prevents you from facing the important question, "Why did my love-relationship have to end?" There are rarely simple answers, so it will take some time and effort. Until you can accept the ending, you will have difficulty adjusting and rebuilding.

chapter two

Owl is crying forlornly in the dark,
I heard him calling to his mate last night.
I waited with him to hear the familiar answering cry,
And my heart fell with his
As the silence fell, louder than a cry.

He is still calling tonight,
Only to be answered by longer silences.
I have never seen the owl.
I have only heard him calling
And waiting...

Nancy

Look at the big crowd gathered at the trailhead waiting to climb the mountain! There are so many kinds of people waiting — all sizes and colors, all ages, both men and women, some wealthy, some poor. Some people think that only people who are *losers* become divorced, but many of these look like winners. Some are eager to start the climb and are doing calisthenics. Some look in shock — as though they have just witnessed a death. There are some who look up the mountain and act overwhelmed, as though they never expect to be able to climb to the top. Many are waiting around, expecting their former love-partners to pick them up so they won't have to make the climb.

Many act confused and disoriented. John is shaking his head and mumbling, "I thought we had a good marriage. I had been the captain of the football team in high school, she was a cheerleader. Everyone predicted we would be perfect together. Then last week she dropped the bombshell on me. She said she was unhappy, that she didn't love me, and she wanted a divorce. She left with our two children to stay with her parents. I was dumbfounded. I thought it would never happen to me."

Mary is impatient to start the climb. She is telling a passerby, "I was so unhappy in our marriage. I wanted a divorce but was afraid to initiate any actions. Then he was killed in a train wreck, and everyone thought I was weird because I felt so little grief. But his death left me free to climb this mountain — when do we start?"

We hear Rita saying, "He has left me and is living with another woman, but I know in my heart that he will always be my husband. God made this marriage and God will have to end it. I refuse to climb this mountain and will stay married until I die. Maybe when we get to Heaven we will be together again."

David is warming his feet by stomping on the ground and appears to be cold and in shock. "I had a good marriage. We never fought. But last night she told me she had fallen in love with my best friend and she was packing her bags to leave. I went in the bathroom and was sick. This morning I called my lawyer and asked him to start divorce proceedings."

Maria is a grey-haired grandmother. "I lived with him and gave him my whole life. I planned to share the harvest of our years in old age with him. But he left without giving any reasons. My harvest is destroyed and I am too old to plant another crop."

I could fill this whole book with stories similar to these. Similar, yet unique stories of people who are reacting in many different ways to the ending of their love-relationship.

It is hard for me or anyone to be comforting when you are hurting so much. The most help I can offer at this point is to listen to your painful words and help you accept the reality of the crisis. You feel as though you have failed, as though you have been hit in the stomach and had your emotional wind knocked out, as though you had just experienced death even though you are still living. The initial shock is easier for those of you who made the decision to leave and who were more prepared for this crisis, but the ending is still painful no matter what the circumstances.

The big question most of you are asking is "Why?" You need to understand what went wrong, to perform an *autopsy* upon the dead relationship. You want to know why, yet denying the pain often prevents you from accepting the results of this emotional autopsy. To understand *why* helps to overcome the denial, so let's discuss some of the reasons love-relationships die.

I like to start my talks to teenagers by asking them, "How many of you plan to get married?" Usually about half of them raise their hands. Then I ask, "How many of you plan to get divorced?" I never see any raised hands after this question.

No one *plans* to get a divorce. And most of us deny it at first if it *does* happen. We want to bury our heads in the sand like ostriches to avoid the storm. But, like the ostrich, we have problems in our love-relationships which are more obvious to others than they are to us.

There are three entities in a love-relationship — two people and the relationship between them. It is analogous to a bridge: the two people are the foundations at each end of the bridge; the relationship is the span which connects these two foundations. When change occurs in one or both of the foundations at the end of the bridge, it strains the bridge itself. Some changes are too great for the bridge to handle, and it falls into the river. In people, such changes may result from personal growth, education, religious experiences, attitude change, anxiety, anger, relocation, or maybe a reaction to stress or trauma. (One way to prevent such stress upon the relationship is to never grow or change — not a very healthy way, is it?) You may recognize that you or your love-partner recently went through a period of change and personal growth, and that this upset the system of interaction in your love-relationship — tumbling your bridge into the river.

If you *need* to doubt and question yourself and your abilities, you may feel that you *should* have been able to adjust to this stress resulting from change. My answer is this: Two of the most important abilities we need to learn in our lives are how to build and maintain this bridge between two people in a love-relationship, and how to parent our children. And where do we receive *education and training* for these two important roles? Mostly in our families — certainly not in school. I was talking to a group of about 100 women recently, and asked them how many would like to have a marriage like that of their parents. There was only *one* that raised her hand! Did the rest receive good training from their families on how to have a happy love-relationship? Did *you* receive good training and education on how to adjust to a strain in your love-relationship?

Perhaps relationship counseling would have helped you to adjust? Perhaps. I state proudly that I am a *terrific* marriage counselor when both parties want to work on the relationship! But I am a lousy marriage counselor when only one wants to work. What was the reality in your love-relationship? Were both you and your partner wanting to work and improve the system, or did only one of you want to work on the relationship? If only one is willing, then it is not very likely that the relationship will improve. A team of horses will not pull a very big load when one of the horses is lying down.

You may be punishing yourself with feelings of failure in your love-relationship by playing the *if only* game: "If only I had listened more; if only I hadn't become so angry; if only I had made love to her every time she wanted to; if only I hadn't been such a bitch."

I hope by now you have satisfied your *need* to punish yourself. I suggest you let it go. Your hindsight is much better now. You have learned a great deal about life and about yourself since the troubles began in your love-relationship. Your awareness and your insights are much improved. How about *using* the new awareness and insight as a basis for further *growth*, rather than self-punishment? Do something for the rest of your life, not the past. Try saying, "I did the best I could with what I knew and what I had to work with," and leave it at that. *Now*, you're going to work on today, and to-morrow, and the next day, and the next....

Maybe your relationship failed because there was a third party involved. It is easier to be angry at that third party than it is to be angry at your former love-partner or yourself. There is a *Catch-22* in being angry at your former love-partner — you are damned if you do, and damned if you don't. How can you be angry at the person you loved? It is easier to be angry at the person who came in and "took your spouse away from you."

There are many reasons why one partner leaves a relationship to become involved with another. You may feel that the other person had something to offer that you did not have. That may be true in some cases. But every love-relationship has some cracks in its foundation, and in many cases — for many reasons — these cracks may result in a breakup. Patterns of development and interaction *start* long before love-relationships end. If there were such serious cracks in your relationship, it may be difficult for you to see and understand them at this time.

Let me give you an example. Many people have not freed themselves from their parents' influence when they marry. They do not have identities of their own, separate from being children of their parents. Such a person may later decide to dump a love-partner. But when you examine what is really going on, you see that he or she is actually dumping the parents' control and influence. To rebel against the spouse may be, in reality, to rebel against the parents.

So the crack in your relationship may have begun even *before* you married. And if there was a crack in your relationship, it is easy for a third party to become involved by filling that crack. It often is easier — or seems easier — for a person outside of the relationship to fill the deficiency than it is for a person who is part of the relationship. A good marriage counselor may be able to help you to explore and understand some of the cracks and deficiencies in your past love-relationship.

Here is another concept to help you understand what went wrong with your relationship. Many people ask, "Why did so-and-so get a divorce?" Sometimes a more relevant question is, "Why did that couple marry?" Many people marry for the wrong reasons, such as 1) to overcome loneliness, 2) to escape an unhappy parental home, 3) because everybody is expected to marry — only *losers* who can't find someone to marry stay single, 4) out of a need to parent another or be parented by another, and the old standby, 5) because "we fell in love."

I will talk more about love in another chapter, but let it suffice for now that there are many levels of love and not all are mature enough to provide a sound basis for getting married. Quite frequently we have an idealized image of that other person. We fell in love with that *image* rather than the person. When the honeymoon is over (a long time passes before reality hits), we are disillusioned because that person is not living up to the image we have idealized. Perhaps "falling in love" is an attempt to fill some of our emptiness, rather than a sound basis on which to build a marriage.

Those who get married for these wrong reasons (including "falling in love") might be described as half people who are trying to become a whole person and find happiness by getting married. Even the usual wedding vows talk about "two people becoming one." During a talk with a group of ministers, one asked if I thought the marriage vows were contributing to divorce. I replied, "Yes." The discussion was lively, and I believe a few of the ministers began to consider changing the vows in the marriage ceremony.

When you are ready to face life alone and have found happiness as a single person, then you are ready to face life together with another person. Two whole people who have climbed the mountain of personal growth and self-awareness will tend to have a much more dynamic relationship than two half people joining together in an attempt to become whole.

Most of the wrong reasons may be summarized by stating that the unhappy person expects that getting married will bring happiness. Do you remember the movies we saw about marriage in the *old days* — the '30s, '40s and '50s? (Television has seen to it that no one is *too young* to remember them!) The movie was all about the *courtship* of the couple. When they married, the movie ended. The subtle message was that you became married and — with no effort — lived happily ever after. Such a fairy tale!

There is another important phenomenon that frequently contributes to the demise of the marriage. Many couples make the mistake of investing all of their time and energy into a project external to the love-relationship. Examples might be building a new house or business, or going to school. This external project may keep the couple so occupied they have little energy or time to invest in their love-relationship. In fact, the project may become a method of avoiding each other. When the house is finished, the couple finds they have nothing in common anymore, and the new house becomes a monument to their divorce.

My son Todd writes his ideas and thoughts on paper and often they are profound. He described a good reason for getting married:

"At some time in the future during my growth toward becoming a full person, there will come a day when my cup runneth over so profusely that the need will arise for another person to soak up the excess."

Recognizing the ending of an unhappy and unproductive relationship may help us look at our divorce as a decision reflecting good mental health.

Take a look at your former relationship, your former partner, and yourself. Set aside for a moment all of *society's* reasons why you were "meant for each other." This is the time for painful honesty. Ask yourself:

Were you and your partner *friends*?

Did you confide in one another?

What interests did you share? Hobbies? Attitudes toward life?
Politics? Religion? Children?

Were your goals — for yourself, each other, the relationship —
similar/compatible?

Did you agree on methods for solving problems between you (not
necessarily the *solutions*, the *methods*)?

When you got angry with each other, did you deal with it directly,
or hide it, or try to hurt each other?

Did you share friendships?

Did you go out together socially?

Did you share responsibilities for earning money and household
chores in a mutually agreed upon way?

Did you make at least major decisions jointly?

Did you allow each other time alone?

Did you trust each other?

Was the relationship important enough for each of you to make
some personal sacrifices for it when necessary?

I hope these questions were not too painful for you. Your honest
answers will probably help you recognize that your relationship
really was — in most cases — at an end, even before the formal sep-
aration/divorce. It is tough to acknowledge some of those short-
comings. It is even tougher to accept that I was part of the problem
(easy enough to blame my partner, or society, or...). Accepting,
however, is the all important *positive* side to this first rebuilding
block called denial.

Take some time with this. And remember: *You do not have to take
on a load of guilt in order to accept that your relationship is over!*
Stay out of the "if only" game. The reasons, the contributing factors are as complex as those structures which support a bridge. It
takes a great deal of analysis of *known* forces and stresses and loads
and strength of materials to build a successful bridge. How infi-
nitely more complex is a successful love-relationship! And how little most of us really *know* about the interpersonal forces and
stresses and loads and strength of our own materials!

You'll learn much more as the journey up our mountain continues. For now, take a deep breath and say it: "My love-relationship
has ended." Now let yourself cry for a while.

Now that you are up to your tears in the reasons why relationships end, and you have taken a hard look at the cracks in your own former love-relationship, you may be feeling "sadder but wiser." And maybe a bit down on yourself. You are not alone at this point either.

A computer taught me a key aspect of learning to accept a love-relationship is ending. On my *Fisher Divorce Adjustment Scale* was a subtest designed to measure how well you had accepted the ending of your love-relationship. When the statistics had been analyzed by the computer, the items of the self-acceptance subtest had disappeared! I checked to find where they had gone, and discovered that many were related to feelings of *self-worth*. The data are clear, and confirmed by others: the better your feelings of self-worth, the easier it is for you to accept the ending of your love-relationship.

If you have difficulty starting the journey up this mountain because you refuse to accept the ending of your love-relationship, you may need to work on improving your self-concept. I know that when you are in the shock of a recent ending, telling you to improve your self-concept is like blowing in the wind — it does not change much. Still, you will find it true. Especially after we deal with self-concept more in chapter eight, you will experience the difference for yourself as you discover more of your own value.

As you come closer to standing alone, to accepting that your relationship has really ended, the emotional pain will get pretty intense. And the pain you are feeling is real. Divorce and death of a spouse are probably the two most painful experiences you will feel in your life. Millions of other people have felt the same things you are feeling as your relationship ends. It hurts. But we need to use our pain to learn. To *flow with* the pain rather than deny it. To use it as motivation to grow and make the crisis into an opportunity, rather than an experience that leaves us with wounds that never heal. We can use the pain as an excuse to remain bitter, angry, unhappy; or we can use the pain to grow. Which do you choose to do?

Those of you who believe that you will be getting back together with your former love-partner probably feel there is no reason to climb this mountain of adjustment. In Colorado about 20 to 30 percent of the people who file for divorce do *not* obtain a final decree (the percentage varies from year to year). We do not know what happens to these couples, but it can be assumed that many resurrect their love-relationship, and get back together again. What is the best plan of action for those of you who want to get back together? Do you have to climb this mountain of adjustment?

If your relationship has become fractured to the point of physical separation and you are talking about divorce, you may need time apart to change the old patterns of interaction. You may need to close off the bridge to traffic while you shore up the foundations. Experience individual personal growth before you start working on the bridge. It is easy just to move in together again, but it is difficult to change the old relationship into something more meaningful and productive without experiencing changes within the two people involved. I think you may need to climb the mountain before you go back to your former love-partner!

I want to become somewhat parental and talk to you about how vulnerable you are to becoming involved in another love-relationship as a way of making your pain go away. My belief is that *you need friends rather than lovers right now*. Have you read Homer's *Odyssey?* The Greek myth tells of sailors on a journey filled with various obstacles. One of these obstacles is an island where there are beautiful female sirens attempting to seduce the sailors into stopping at their island (the sailors have been forewarned that stopping will lead to their destruction). They prevent the sirens from tempting them by tying themselves to the mast and blindfolding themselves. You will need to tie yourself to the mast of self-discipline and avoid becoming too deeply involved in another love-relationship until you have healed some of the emotional pain. Almost always a relationship started when you are in deep pain will add to your misery in the long run. But friendships are helpful; and if you can build friendships rather than love-relationships, it will be more productive, for the present.

Imagine a circus tightrope act. The platform at one end represents the security you had in the love-relationship. The platform at the other end represents the inner security you need to find within yourself. You need to walk across the tightrope in your adjustment process to find that inner security. You can fall off one side by withdrawing into your apartment or home and not making any friends.

You can fall off the other side by becoming deeply involved in another long-term, committed love-relationship — if you are emotionally investing more in the relationship than you are investing in your own personal growth. You wake up one morning and discover you are trying to please the other person and trying to make the relationship work, but you are not trying to become the person you wish to be.

The balance pole is having friends that help you keep your balance as you walk across the tightrope. They give you honest feedback that is not biased by a need to have your love. Friends are more objective than lovers, and you need objectivity at this point in your life. Set yourself a goal: learn to be happy as a single person before you become coupled again!

About the **children**: There are three areas relating to self-acceptance that cause problems for kids. Number one is that children of divorce will continue to maintain some sort of a fantasy image of their parents getting back together again, with much emotional investment in that dream. They have difficulty accepting the reality that their parents' relationship is over. It may be a surprise to learn how strong this fantasy is in your children. You continually need to present them with the reality that the relationship is over, so they do not continue to invest in this fantasy. Kids may use all kinds of manipulative behavior trying to get the two of you back together again, trying to have you spend time together, or trying to get you talking to each other. Be aware of the large emotional investment your kids have in *not* accepting the ending of their parents' relationship and in hoping that their parents will get back together again. Respond gently but firmly and persistently with your own decision — that the marriage is over.

An important second aspect with kids and self-acceptance is their belief that they did something to *cause* their parents' breakup. The last time that they disobeyed — when they did not go to bed or clean up their food at mealtime or do their household chores — they think this led to their parents' fight and then to their divorce. Try hard to help your kids see that it is not their fault and that divorce is a grown-up problem.

A third aspect has to do with the fear that now the children have

lost one parent, will they lose the other parent? They tend to be very
clinging and dependent upon the parents, and they need a lot of reassurance that the parents will not leave. Parents do divorce each
other, but they do not divorce their children. You need to reassure
your children that even though Mom and Dad are divorced from
each other, they will never divorce the children.

The crowd at the trailhead grows restless to continue the journey.
Some of you will make this journey even though you do not want to,
even though you are still married in your heart. The emotional pain
is so great that you know you have to climb. It will benefit you to
learn as much from this journey as possible, so decide to make it a
positive experience, rather than a begrudging one.

Here is this chapter's checklist, designed to help you decide if you
are ready to climb the next portion of the trail. Use it to check out
your progress. No one is *grading* you, so be very honest with
yourself.

1. *I am able to accept that my love-relationship is ending.*
2. *I am comfortable telling my friends and relatives that my love-relationship is ending.*
3. *I have begun to understand some of the reasons why my love-relationship did not work out, and this has helped me overcome the feelings of denial.*
4. *I believe that even though divorce is painful, it can be a positive and creative experience.*
5. *I am ready to invest emotionally in my own personal growth in order to become the person I would like to be.*
6. *I want to learn to become happy as a single person before committing myself to another love-relationship.*
7. *I will continue to invest in my own personal growth even if my former love-partner and I plan to get back together.*

From LONELINESS to Aloneness

 It is natural to feel extreme loneliness when your love-relationship ends. But healing can come from the pain, if you listen to it. You can learn how to grow through loneliness to the stage of aloneness — where you are comfortable being by yourself.

chapter three

Loneliness is a disease
That grows slowly and
Undetected. Its symptoms
Are terrifying.
Loneliness is a dark,
Unseeing veil that covers
You with sadness, and a
Desperate race to conquer the
Complete spiritual and
Emotional emptiness...

I am experiencing this
Disease, and wish I could
Find a cure —
But even a ray of sunlight
Is a blessed thing.
For loneliness demands; it takes
Everything from you and
In return gives you nothing
But solitude; as if you
Were the only person
In an unmerciful world.

Elaine

As we look around and watch people climbing this mountain of rebuilding blocks, we see various kinds of loneliness. There are the people who have withdrawn into their cave and just peer out sullenly, looking very sad and dejected. And there are the lonely people who insist on being with somebody else, so they always are holding hands or following somebody around. And then there are the busy people — always busy doing this and that so they never have to face their loneliness.

Loneliness is pain. But it is a pain which tells us we have something important to learn.

Loneliness can be a vacuum or an iceberg. Lonely people need to deal with the vacuum inside by sucking up everyone around in order to fill their void. Or they need to deal with the iceberg inside by trying to gain warmth from everyone around.

The formerly married do not have a corner on the loneliness market. Untold numbers suffer from the affliction. For many, it began in childhood and persisted through the marriage and into divorce. (Another cause of divorce, for those of you who are keeping a list.) This may be a crucial part of the climb for you if loneliness has been a stumbling block for years.

The loneliness that comes when that special person is gone is often more intense than any we have ever felt. We have no one with whom to share meals, bed, or the special comments and behavior of our children. Used to having the sounds, smells, and touch of that other person in the home, we now know nothing but silence. There is a strange emptiness in the house, as though a gong was struck and produced no sound. We can find no one in the whole world for us to see, hear, or feel as we do. Friends who do try to reach out seem distant, even as we most need them to be close and real.

Voices within scream, "Withdraw, withdraw, and you won't be hurt again!" We want seclusion, but at the same time crave emotional warmth, like the wounded dog who retires to parts unknown until its wound is healed. We want to regress to childhood, to have a mommy care for us.

Some who are lonely in marriage, suddenly are relieved to end the relationship that encouraged loneliness. Never emotionally close to our beloved, we found life with that person painful. Whatever kept us from closeness was hard to understand and harder to change. The negative feelings of pain, anger, and frustration toward that person may have led to keeping distance between us. Ending the relationship gained distance while avoiding the painful expression of those negative feelings. (Another cause of divorce — are you keeping track?)

Many of the rebuilding blocks have a three-stage pattern. For *loneliness*, the first stage is withdrawal; one may withdraw or fantasize about it. Some hide in empty apartments and brood, so that others will not suspect our fear. Another approach is to play the "poor-little-me" game, hoping that someone will come along and feel sorry. The goal is to keep others from seeing how much one hurts, while at the same time letting the former partner know.

Quiet is a constant reminder during this stage that the other person is gone — really gone. The silence can be crushing. Inability to concentrate makes reading impossible. TV is boring. Nothing is exciting! There is a nagging, restless desire to do something — but what?

Withdrawal may be *appropriate* for some during this period because — let's face it — we are not very good company. The need for emotional warmth is insatiable. The need often stifles friends, engulfs them, and denies them space to be themselves, to be *friends*. I am reminded of a nursery story about millions and billions and trillions of cats who began to eat each other up until there were no cats left. Close friends in this stage can "eat each other up" until there is nothing left of either!

Life is often like a pendulum, swinging from one extreme to the other. Seeking ways to escape this loneliness, many of us enter a second stage, becoming *busyholics*, with an activity for each night of the week and two activities for each night of the weekend. We work long hours at our jobs and find all kinds of excuses to keep working rather than coming home to the lonely apartment. (We also may have been *workaholics* while married — perhaps to keep from coming home to a lonely marriage.) We go out with people whom we really do not enjoy just to avoid being alone. A party for singles may last all night — no one wants to go home!

We are running from ourselves — as though a frightening ghost lurked inside, a ghost of loneliness. For those who have really been lonely, the ghost may have begun to seem real! We never take time to stop and look at what we are doing or where we are going because we are so busy running. Instead of climbing up the mountain, we are running around it in circles!

This *busy-loneliness* varies in length and intensity from person to person. Some may only feel that they want to be busy; others may become so busy that they have to walk on tiptoes to keep their posteriors from dragging. Eventually all get tired and begin to realize that there must be more to life than running from the ghost of loneliness. Then they begin to slow down into the *aloneness* stage.

Aloneness — what one friend called the "all-oneness" stage — is achieved at the point of being *comfortable* by yourself. You may *choose* to be at home alone by the fire with a book, rather than going out to be with people you really do not like. Development of inner resources and personality leads to interests, activities, thoughts, and attitudes that make it comfortable to be alone with oneself.

"How do I get there from here?" Start by facing the ghost of loneliness and realizing that it is a ghost! You have run from it, feared it, avoided it. But when you turn to that ghost of loneliness and say "Boo!" often the ghost loses its power and control. You have accepted loneliness as part of being human, and thereby become more comfortable being alone.

Accept also that loneliness has healing qualities. A period of time alone with oneself allows introspection, reflection, growth and development of the inner self. Hollowness and emptiness are replaced by inner fullness and strength. You have made a giant step toward *independence* when you are comfortable by yourself, no longer dependent on the company of others.

Choosing to be with another person *to escape loneliness* is a very unhealthy reason to begin another love-relationship. There is tremendous therapeutic value in being by yourself, even lonely for a time, before you start another love-relationship. Time really is the best healer. A period of loneliness is part of the remedy you need so that you can *choose* to enter into the next relationship rather than *needing* the next relationship to overcome loneliness. The mentally healthy person maintains a balance between being with others and being alone. You need to find what the proper balance is for you.

Children suffer loneliness too after their parents are divorced. They have the same kind of empty feelings inside them that the parents have. They have the same need to be with others to fill up that loneliness, but they also fear being close to others.

Kids may feel they are the only divorced kid in school. In one community, divorce was so prevalent that when one youngster told school friends that his parents were getting a divorce, the other kids said, "Your parents are finally getting with it, aren't they?" In another community, divorce can still be so "wrong," so unusual, that the child might *be* the only divorced kid in the grade.

Daily living habits are altered just as are those of the parents. Instead of coming home and having two parents to spend time with them, play with them, put them to bed, there is only one parent. And the kids feel the loneliness of the new house when one or both parents move. At the home of the noncustodial parent, there may not be familiar toys or books to play with. Often the other parent's home is not set up for children, and may be located in a new neighborhood, away from friends.

The kids need to work through this loneliness — just as the parents do — in order to develop their own healthy feelings of aloneness. Kids need to learn that they have the resources within themselves to spend time alone without having to have another person around.

Many kids may have been lonely before the divorce because the interaction within the family did not help them to feel that they belonged. Divorce tends to increase this feeling of not belonging or not being okay. However, perhaps the crisis itself can be used to help deal directly with the problem. It is a special time for parents to help the children feel that they belong, that they are loved, and that they are an important part of this new family — whether it be a single-parent family or a two-parent family with the parents living apart.

Nevertheless, as with all of the rebuilding blocks, when the parents are dealing with their own loneliness, it is very difficult for them to have enough emotional time and energy left to devote to the kids' needs. It may be necessary, as I mentioned before, for parents to work through their own rebuilding blocks first; then they will be better able to help their children.

Do some work *now* on your own capacity for being alone. If you can honestly answer ''yes'' to most of the items listed below, you have developed a healthy *aloneness*, and you are ready to move on up the mountain. If more than three or four of these areas need work, spend some time going over this chapter, so you can become more comfortable being by yourself.

1. *I am taking time for myself rather than keeping too busy.*
2. *I am not working such long hours that I have no time for myself.*
3. *I am not hiding from loneliness by being with people I don't enjoy being with.*
4. *I have begun to fill up my time with activities important to me.*
5. *I have stopped hiding and withdrawing into my home or apartment.*
6. *I have stopped trying to find another love-relationship just to avoid being lonely.*
7. *I am content doing activities by myself.*
8. *I have stopped running from loneliness.*
9. *I am not letting the feelings of loneliness control my behavior.*
10. *I am comfortable being alone and having aloneness time.*

GUILT vs. REJECTION:
Dumpers 1, Dumpees 0

Dumpers end the love-relationship, while dumpees have it ended for them. The adjustment process differs since dumpers feel more guilt and dumpees feel more rejection. Dumpers start their adjustment while still in the love-relationship, but dumpees start adjusting later. For the mutuals, people who jointly decide to end the relationship, the adjustment process is somewhat easier.

chapter four

I laughed so hard...
It was the funniest joke I ever heard;
"He doesn't love you."
And it was even funnier
When you told it yourself;
"I don't love you."
And I laughed so hard
That the whole house shook,
And came crashing down upon me.

Nancy

As we begin this segment of our climb through the rebuilding blocks, let me explain where we are headed in the pages ahead. The four key concepts of this chapter are so closely intertwined that it may get confusing at times. We will be viewing the two main characters in the divorce drama as *dumper* and *dumpee*. And we will take a look at two of the very strong feelings which accompany the trauma of divorce — <u>guilt</u> and <u>rejection</u>.

We notice different groups of people on this portion of the trail. There are those who are in shock, lying on the ground trying to get their emotional wind back. Some are walking around looking guilty and trying not to look at those on the ground. Then there are others who are walking around holding hands with their former lovers! (What are *they* doing here, anyway?) Everyone looks sad.

On the ground are the *dumpees*, who were walking the pathway of life and enjoying their love-relationships when their partners announced they were leaving. Sometimes the dumpees had some warning; sometimes they had none. They have a great deal of difficulty accepting the ending of their relationships.

Those looking guilty are the *dumpers*. They had been thinking about leaving the relationship for some time, maybe a year or two, trying to get their courage up because they knew it would hurt the dumpee a great deal. They avoid looking at the dumpees because that makes them feel more guilty. They are usually better climbers because they had been thinking about the climb while still in the love-relationship.

43

The ones holding hands — the *mutuals* — have decided jointly to end the relationship. Notice how few of them there are! Many people ask them why they are ending the relationship if they are such good friends. They may be very unhappy *together*, and want to end the relationship for the benefit of both. They are good climbers because they do not keep tripping each other as often as the dumpers and dumpees do. Mutuals do not enjoy the game going on between dumpers and dumpees: ''Keep-the-other-from-climbing-faster-than-me.''

To get us started up this portion of the trail, here is an over-simplified summary of the chapter. *Dumpers are the partners who leave the relationship, and they often feel considerable guilt; dumpees are the partners who want to hang on to the relationship, and they often experience strong feelings of rejection.* Of course it is not really as simple as that! We will get into much more detail in the pages ahead, but that gives you a map for the area we are about to enter.

Nearly everyone has been a *dumpee* in some relationship, and no one enjoys rejection. I find after being rejected I become very introspective, continually examining myself to see what fault causes people to reject me. Such a self-examination can help me see myself more clearly — perhaps I will *want* to change the way I relate to other people. In any case, to accept the fact that feeling rejected is an expected part of the ending of a relationship — particularly a love-relationship — is helpful in itself.

One step toward overcoming those feelings of rejection is to learn that the breakup of the love-relationship perhaps is not my fault. Everyone brings much of the past into a love-relationship, a past which often determines the course of events in the relationship. Because the love-relationship ended does not necessarily mean that I am inadequate or inferior or that there is something wrong with me. Relationships do end. Maybe that ending is not an indication of inadequacy at all!

The goal is to say, ''If we have a problem, it's not because there is something terribly wrong with me. If we can't work it out, then he (she) has as much to lose as I have — maybe more.'' Feeling that good about yourself is a difficult goal to reach emotionally. Do not be discouraged if it takes quite a period of time to admit that the responsibility is *mutual*, not yours or your ex-partner's alone!

You are a worthwhile person, capable of loving and being loved! You have something special to offer to others, and that is your own unique individual self. You really ought to believe that! You could even get to feeling so good about yourself that you might believe that anyone who dumps such a neat person must have a problem!

Let us look now at guilt. It may sound strange, but I think the ideal may well be to have "the right amount of guilt in your personality." If you feel no guilt at all, nothing other than being caught deters you from doing harmful things to yourself or to others. A sense of guilt is helpful in making decisions about the way one chooses to live. Unfortunately, many people experience so much guilt that they become very inhibited and controlled, unable to do the productive things which can bring happiness. The happy balance is "just enough" guilt to help maintain a sense of direction without severely restricting one's options.

Ending a love-relationship tends to make one deal realistically with guilt feelings. The dumper especially, feels a large amount of guilt and says, "I'm feeling very bad about hurting somebody I love, or used to love, and I wish I could meet *my* needs without feeling so guilty." Guilt — or the tendency to feel it — appears to be deeply ingrained in the personality and it is difficult to overcome. The best solution appears to be rational thinking about the breakup: Listen to your head right now, not your heart (and its guilt feelings!). To end a love-relationship may be *appropriate* because it has been destructive for *both* people. Under those conditions, instead of sitting around feeling guilty, those involved may be able to say, "This is probably the best decision for both of us."

One way to resolve guilt is to be punished. Once when I was teaching, I marched a misbehaving seventh-grade boy to the hall and gave him such a lecture that he began crying. I then felt somewhat mean and hurtful. After school that day, much to my surprise, he came to my room and acted as though I was his long lost friend. I realized that by punishing him, I helped him overcome his guilt, and he appreciated that. When we are feeling guilty, we often seek ways of punishing ourselves to relieve the guilt. If you see you are trying to punish yourself by setting yourself up to experience pain in relationships, maybe you should look for feelings of guilt which may be motivating your behavior.

Guilt is usually a result of not living up to some standard of behavior. If the standard is one you have freely chosen for yourself, and if it is a *possible* one, it is probably healthy to feel some guilt about falling short. But if the standard is someone else's, or society's, or the church's, and not one you have adopted for your own, your guilt feelings are not productive. Give yourself a break! It is tough enough to live up to *your own* standards, you can't expect to please *everyone*!

"But," you tell me ruefully, "staying married *is* one of *my* standards. I feel guilty because I didn't make the marriage work, so I failed one of my own standards." I hear you, and I understand that feeling. What I hope for you is that you can come to accept your own *humanness*. Nobody is perfect! Maybe you could take another look at that feeling of guilt, and consider a more useful response to the situation.

Try this one on for size: "My love-partner and I aren't able to make our love-relationship meet our needs and provide us happiness. It appears that, somehow or another, we didn't learn enough about interacting with another person." I remember in school taking a test that I hadn't prepared for. Well, I did poorly on the test, and felt bad. But I didn't fail the whole course! As an adult, I feel bad because my love-relationship didn't work. Maybe I can learn from this experience so I can do better the next time. I might even help my ex learn something positive. Maybe, if I can accept my guilt as appropriate for this situation, then I can change myself into a better person who could build a productive, meaningful relationship in the future, if I so choose.

I want to compare *appropriate* guilt to the large reservoir of guilt that seems to be *free-floating* within our feelings and personalities. Appropriate guilt is when we do something wrong or do something to hurt somebody, and we feel badly about it. When a love-relationship ends, it is very appropriate for us to feel badly about hurting somebody else or hurting ourselves. Appropriate guilt is simply a process that we will work through.

However, some of us have long-standing guilt, usually from childhood, that is a large reservoir of guilty feelings waiting to be released. Some event will come along and tap this reservoir of guilt. Then we will suddenly feel so guilty that we will feel anxious, afraid, and fearful. The guilt is overwhelming because it does not seem to be attached to anything or related to anything. It just feels huge and enormous. If we have this sort of free-floating guilt within us, we may need help from therapy to cut down and minimize the guilt and get it under control. Again, maybe the crisis of divorce will motivate us to work on something we have needed to do for a long time.

Acceptance is an important aspect of dealing with rejection and guilt. In the seminars, the emotional atmosphere is that of acceptance of one's own feelings, and a feeling of emotional support. Being with people who make us feel accepted and supported heals feelings of rejection rapidly. If you can find warm, supportive, accepting friends, you will be able to heal feelings of rejection also.

Rejection and guilt are also closely tied to feelings of self-worth and self-love, which we will discuss in later chapters. You will find that as you improve your feelings of self-worth and self-love, you will be less devastated by rejection.

In my classes approximately one-half of the people state that they were dumpees, one-third state they were dumpers, and the rest state it was a mutual decision. I have no way of knowing if this is true of the general population. Presumably there would be an equal number of dumpers and dumpees in society. However, in some situations, one person feels like a dumpee, and the other person feels it was a mutual decision.

The divorce process is different in many ways for dumpers and dumpees. My research with the *Fisher Divorce Adjustment Scale* indicates that dumpees experience more emotional pain at the point of separation, especially in the areas of letting go and anger. However, if dumpers' pain could be measured while they were still in the love-relationship, I am certain they would show *more* emotional pain than the dumpees. The dumpers began to let go before they left the relationship, so they have been able to back off from being lovers to being friends with the dumpees. The dumpee, however, is usually still deeply in love with the dumper when the relationship ends. (Mutuals tend to score like dumpers, but they experience less grief.)

Occasionally there are persons who have a strong negative reaction to the words "dumper" and "dumpee." They fail to see any humor in the words. They usually have not been able to accept

their divorce, and definitely have not been able to accept the idea of
being a dumper or a dumpee. Despite such strong reactions, I consider it good to use the terms because we each need to accept the
reality of a dumper and a dumpee in nearly every dissolution. You
can climb the mountain of rebuilding more rapidly if you accept your
role.

You may not know if you are a dumper or a dumpee. First of all,
you may not have thought about it. Second, the roles may switch
back and forth. For example, George and Margaret were childhood
sweethearts who married soon after graduating from high school.
During the courtship and marriage, George was continually
stepping out with other women, leaving home for short periods of
time, and acting like a dumper wanting out of the relationship.
Finally, Margaret reached her ''martyr's tolerance limit'' and filed
for divorce. Immediately George's behavior and vocabulary became
those of a dumpee. Margaret and George had switched roles.

Language is a clue to whether you are a dumper or dumpee.
When I talk to an audience, I frequently can identify someone as a
dumper or dumpee just by the question he or she asks. Questioners
are surprised and wonder if I am a mind reader, until I explain that
there are dumper and dumpee vocabularies.

Dumper vocabulary goes like this: ''I need some time and space
to get my head on straight. I need to be out of this relationship in
order to get this time and space. I care for you, but don't love you
enough to live with you. Don't ask me why I don't love you — I just
know that I need out. I feel badly for hurting you, but there is
nothing I can do about that because staying with you would also hurt
you. Can we be friends?''

Dumpee vocabulary goes like this: ''Please don't leave me! Why
don't you love me? Tell me what is wrong with me and I will change.
There must be something wrong with me, and I don't know what it
is. Please tell me what I did wrong. I thought we had a good love-
relationship and I don't see why you want to leave. Please give me
some more time before you leave. I want to be friends but I love you.
Please don't leave me.''

The dumper may reply: ''I have been trying for a long time to tell
you that I was unhappy in the relationship and that we needed to
change. You just wouldn't listen. I have tried everything. I don't

have any more time. You keep hanging onto me and I just want to be friends.''

Dumpees at this point are likely to be hurt and to cry. They become introspective and try to understand what went wrong: ''Why am I unlovable?'' and ''Why did our relationship have to end?'' Often there is denial of feelings while the dumpee gains time to recover from the shock. The emotional pain is great for the dumpee at this point.

The vocabulary seems universal; almost all dumpers and dumpees use the same words. The problem of *timing* is evident. The dumper claims to have been trying for ''months and years'' to do something about the problem, during much of that time thinking about leaving. The dumpee has not heard this dissatisfaction, perhaps because he or she had started using denial long before the dumper actually left. But when the dumper makes the announcement, the dumpee really starts denying and refusing to believe there is anything wrong. ''We had such a *good* relationship!''

Notice the difference in *priorities*. The dumper wants to work on *personal growth*: ''I have to get my head on straight.'' The dumpee wants to work on the *relationship*: ''I need more time and feedback about what I need to change.'' Listen carefully to the words the dumpee is saying to reflect the hurt. Can you hear the anger beneath the words? But the dumpee does not express these words because the divorce is still in its *honeymoon period*.

During this period, the dumper is feeling much guilt, acting super nice, willing to give the dumpee anything. The dumpee is feeling rejected, anxious for the dumper to come back, and afraid to express anger for fear it will drive the dumper even further away. The dumpee is acting super nice also. Eventually anger replaces the feelings of guilt in the dumper and the feelings of rejection in the dumpee. Then the honeymoon period ends. This phase often begins around three months after the separation, but the timing may vary a great deal. ''Good court settlements'' are often negotiated while dumpers feel so guilty they will give up everything, and while dumpees will settle for anything in hopes of getting the dumper back. Dumpers: ''I want out so badly that I don't care about property or money.'' Dumpees: ''I won't ask for anything because all I want is for her (him) to come back.''

There is a strategy to change the honeymoon period in case you are interested. Both parties feel better and can speed up the adjustment process when the dumpee can express anger quicker. Dumpers feel less guilty when dumpees express anger because the anger helps them deal with guilt. And dumpees feel less depression by expressing anger quicker because some depression is repressed anger. But it is not always possible to shortcut the process because the dumper may have a need to feel guilty for a while, and the dumpee may have a need to feel rejected and depressed for a while. Working through feelings takes time.

There is an exercise that will help you to understand this dumper-dumpee concept better. Find a friend to role-play with you — one of you as dumper, the other as dumpee. Begin in the middle of a room, then have the *dumper* walk out of the room saying dumper vocabulary. The *dumpee* should follow after, trying to keep the dumper from leaving the room by using dumpee vocabulary and behavior. Change roles so you can experience being both a dumper and a dumpee.

The symbolism of the exercise is good. The dumper is looking toward the door and trying to get out. The dumpee is looking at the back of the dumper and trying to figure out a way to prevent the leaving. (I have known dumpees who follow the partner out of the room, out to the car, and then hang on the car as the dumper drives off.)

How does it feel to be a dumper in the exercise? Did you feel guilty? Did you feel the other person was hanging onto you to keep you from leaving? Did you feel reluctant to look back at the other person? Did you try to keep looking at the door? Did you feel like walking faster or maybe even running?

How does it feel to be a dumpee in the exercise? Did you want the other person to look at you? Did you feel the desire to physically grab the other person? Did you want to cry and plead with him/her not to leave? Did you feel rejection and loneliness as the other person left the room? Did you feel anger?

At the risk of confusing this discussion further, I want to introduce a further breakdown in the dumper-dumpee categories. The words I am going to use are strong and somewhat judgmental, but they are helpful in understanding better the dumper-dumpee concept. There are *good-dumpers* and *bad-dumpers*, and *good-dumpees* and *bad-dumpees*.

The good-dumper is a person who has tried to work on the love-relationship in order to make it last. A good-dumper was willing to make changes, invest emotionally in trying to change, and go for marriage counseling if appropriate. But finally the dumper realized that the relationship was destructive to both people, and that it is better to end an unhealthy relationship than to continue to destroy each other. This person has the courage and strength to end the relationship, and it often takes a great deal of courage and strength.

Bad-dumpers are very similar to runaway kids. They believe the grass is greener on the other side of the fence, and all that is needed for happiness is to get out of the relationship. There is often another love-relationship waiting in the wings. The bad-dumper avoids dealing with feelings and avoids looking inside at attitudes that might need to be changed. Bad-dumpers often leave quickly without even a "goodbye" conversation or explanation of their intent to end the partnership.

Good-dumpees are open, honest, willing to work on the relationship, and willing to go for counseling if appropriate. They seldom have had an affair, and have likely worked hard on communicating. They are not "innocent victims" in the sense that they too have done things to hurt the relationship. They are basically at the wrong time and place when the internal explosion and the need to be out of the relationship take place in the dumper.

Bad-dumpees are people who want out of the relationship but do not have the courage and strength to be a dumper. They make it miserable for the other person who then is forced into being the dumper.

There are few who fit perfectly into these four categories. Most of us are a combination of both good and bad dumpers or dumpees.

It may occur to you to ask if the person who files for dissolution in court is the dumper. The person who files may or may not be the dumper; filing is not the deciding factor. And you may ask if there are more male or female dumpers. Of course I have no way of knowing about the general population, but in my classes there is exactly the same percentage of male and female dumpers!

Another important phenomenon in the dumper-dumpee relationship is the "pain cycle." The dumper is not hurting as much when the relationship ends, but the dumpee's pain is great and motivates rapid growth and adjustment. When the dumpee is reaching a good emotional adjustment, the dumper frequently comes back and begins talking about reconciliation. This really blows the dumpee away. Gordon exclaimed, "I devoted all my emotional energy to learning to accept the ending of the relationship and I'd given up completely the hope that Juanita would come back. And then she called me!"

There are many different ways to interpret this phenomenon: Perhaps the dumper, in contrast to the sense of euphoria when she/he first left, has found it so scary out there in the single world that the security of the old love-relationship looks good. "There ain't nothing out there but turkeys, and the old lover looks better all the time." Another interpretation is illustrated by dumpee anger, "She made me the dumpee. Now she wants to make me the dumper, to share the guilt!" Perhaps the best explanation comes from observing that the dumper comes back around the time the dumpee is "making it" successfully. Maybe when Juanita no longer felt the guilt and responsibility of having Gordon cling with dependency, she felt free to come back into a more equal relationship.

The typical dumpee reaction is not to take the dumper back. Dumpees find that they can make it on their own, that being single has advantages, and that it feels good to experience the personal growth they have been experiencing. If you get a dumpee to talk long enough, you will learn what was wrong with the relationship. It is only during the first period of denial that the dumpee maintains there was nothing wrong with the relationship. "Now I can see what was happening all those years! Besides, I don't see that much change and personal growth in Juanita, so why should I want the old relationship back?" At this point the dumper usually gets dumped!

The concept of dumper and dumpee has interesting complications for the **children** of divorce. Often the children are very angry at the parent who decided to leave, and they have a great deal of difficulty maintaining a relationship with that person. They blame the break-up on the dumper, so they take out their pain and frustration on that person. They probably fail to see that there is not that much difference between the dumper and dumpee, since both of them contributed to the ending of the relationship, only in different ways.

Almost always, the children of divorce could be looked upon as dumpees. They had very little to do with the decision, thus may feel the same frustration and anger that dumpees do. Kids, however, are *not* like dumpees in the sense that they often recognize that the marriage is ending — sometimes before the parents do!

Kids have a definite problem with rejection and guilt. I mentioned in chapter one that kids may have problems with guilt when they feel they are responsible for their parents' marriage not working out. The youngsters may need help in seeing that it is not their fault, that divorce is a grown-up problem.

Kids frequently feel a tremendous amount of rejection because it seems one parent is leaving and rejecting the child. The rejection that the child feels often is long lasting and can even persist into adulthood. Adults who have never fully accepted their parents' divorce find that their own love-relationships can be adversely affected.

Children need to realize that *they* are not guilty for their parents' divorce, and *they* are not being rejected. If the parents can maintain a quality relationship with the children after their separation and divorce, the children will be able to deal with these feelings.

It is no wonder that dumpers and dumpees have trouble working together! The *timing* is different, with the dumper often starting the adjustment process while still in the relationship. The *feelings* are different, with the dumper tending to feel more guilt and the dumpee tending to feel more rejection (although you may experience both, whether you were a dumper or a dumpee). The *attitudes* are different for the two people because the dumper feels pressure to leave the relationship (wanting "personal growth" of some sort), and the dumpee fears the relationship ending. The dumper has already let go much more than the dumpee, causing problems in communicating and interacting. These different attitudes and behaviors add to the trauma of adjusting to the ending of a love-relationship.

One last note on the terms *dumper* and *dumpee*. Despite differences in timing and attitudes, the two *people* are not that much different. Both have contributed fairly equally to the relationship not working. Even differences in their attitudes are not major. Once a dumpee begins talking about the love-relationship, he or she will say almost the same things about the problems that the dumper was saying, using dumpee vocabulary of course. *Timing* remains the essential element that separates the dumper from the dumpee.

I hope this discussion of dumpers and dumpees will enable you to see that feelings of guilt and rejection are part of the process. Intellectual understanding is often the first step of awareness that leads to emotional understanding. Feelings of guilt and rejection are normal and typical during the ending of a love-relationship — in fact you may have been experiencing these feelings before. But the ending of a love-relationship tends to magnify and emphasize feelings, so you can be more aware of them and thus learn to deal with them more adequately.

I suggest we rest from our climb for a while. You may want to think about the differences between dumpers and dumpees, and try to understand the feelings and attitudes on both sides of the issue. Maybe you have changed your mind about whether you are a dumper or a dumpee after reading this chapter. In any case, take time now to consider the different perspectives partners get of *what happened* during a dissolution. I hope this chapter has helped you gain a better view of the end of your own relationship. After completing the check list below and treating yourself to some time to think about these ideas, I hope you are then ready to move on up the mountain!

1. *I am no longer overwhelmed by feelings of guilt and/or rejection.*
2. *I can accept that I was a dumper or a dumpee or that we made a mutual decision.*
3. *I have thought about whether I was a good/bad dumper/ dumpee.*
4. *I can accept that being a dumper may not necessarily mean one should feel guilty.*
5. *I can accept that being a dumpee may not necessarily mean one should feel rejected and unlovable.*
6. *I am aware of the differences in feelings and behavior between dumpers and dumpees.*

7. I realize that both dumpers and dumpees feel emotional pain even though it may differ in timing and intensity.
8. I understand that in some areas I was a dumper and in other areas I was a dumpee, since this is typical of most relationships.
9. I understand the concept of dumper/dumpee is most meaningful at the point of separation; as I grow it becomes less and less important.
10. I have looked at my life patterns to see if rejection or guilt feelings have controlled much of my behavior.
11. I am working to overcome the influence of rejection and guilt in my life.

GRIEF: Big Boys – and Girls – Do Cry

Grief is an important part of your divorce process. You need to work through grief's emotions in order to let go of the dead love-relationship. An intellectual grasp of the stages of grief can help you become emotionally aware of grief. Then you can do the grieving that you may have been afraid of before.

chapter five

Weekends are...
All the lonely hours poured into remembering,
All the lonely thoughts poured into trying to forget,
The harder we try to forget, the easier it is to remember,
The past can't die and the future can't live,
But the present exists.

If silence is deafening, then what is quiet?
Quiet is weekends and weekends are hell.
Wake up and face reality — why?
Weekends enforce reality, weekdays subdue it.

Saturday — it's a world of two plus two,
Where one has no meaning and no value.
Sunday — the body rests,
But where's the "off" button for the mind?

"Honey"

We are now entering one of the most difficult and emotionally draining parts of the climb. All along the path sit people who are crying mournfully. Some will stop crying for a while, then suddenly start in again. Other people are trying to comfort them, but seem uncomfortable and not quite sure what to do. What is happening?

These people are experiencing grief. Whenever there is a loss of something important in our lives, we suffer grief. Perhaps you — like many of the people participating in the divorce seminar — had not been aware that grieving is a part of the divorce process. For death, there is a set ritual with a funeral, casket, and acceptance that grieving is important. For divorce, there is no prescribed ritual other than the court hearing, and grief is often not acknowledged or accepted. But, the death of a love-relationship is cause for us to grieve!

Many forms of loss occur when we end a love-relationship. Most obvious of course is the loss of the love-partner, which many people *do* grieve. There are other losses: the future plans as a pair; the love-relationship; the role of *husband* or *wife* or *lover*; and the status associated with being a *couple*. Many changes occur as one progresses from being married through the transition to being single. For some people the loss of the *relationship* is as important as the loss of the *partner*.

There is the loss of the future. Married "till death do us part," there were plans, goals, joint careers, and a house that had become a home. Now all of these future parts of your life are no longer there. The future is a very difficult loss to accept, and many will need to grieve that loss for a long time.

The pain of ending a love-relationship often forces us to look at past pain. Many people have not properly grieved a loss in the past, such as the death of a loved one. Re-experiencing a past pain intensifies the grieving process. For those who carry an unresolved loss from the past, divorce grief will be especially painful and difficult.

Similarly, a history of unfulfilled emotional needs — perhaps childhood deprivations — may become prominent during divorce grief. Dan reported that he dreamed frequently about childhood experiences on the farm while he was working through his divorce. As we talked about grief in the seminar, he realized that he was grieving the unhappiness he experienced during his lonely childhood.

Many divorced people are forced to move from the house they lived in while in the love-relationship, and they may have to grieve the loss of that house. Single parents may have to grieve the loss of children when they are with the other parent. And the children must also grieve the loss of a house, a parent, a family — which are all part of their divorce process.

A favorite device of mine, useful in understanding grief, is known as the *check mark theory*. It goes like this:

Once upon a time, there was a little creature called Jot, living a good life, oblivious to the Black Cloud hovering over it. Suddenly, the Black Cloud let loose, and Jot's lover went away. In the anguish of its lost love, Jot tumbled down a huge slide, so long that Jot could not see the bottom of it. There were no handles to hold on the way down the scary slide, and the ride was painful, but Jot finally landed on a soft rainbow. Looking around, Jot spied stairs that led up into the sunlight again. The stairs were very difficult to climb at first, but became easier and more exciting as Jot neared the sunshine and began to feel completely renewed.

You might like to know what Jot's trip was like, since you will have to take the grief trip someday.

I hurt. This looks like a tough climb!

Why me? Wow, it's a long way up, but I'm gaining strength.

I'm so lonely. Maybe I'll slow down to catch my breath.

I'm so unlovable. It's great to have a few friends to help out.

Won't someone hold me? I'm going to make it.

Sadness is my only friend. Look at the new me.

I sigh a lot. I'm OK — you're OK.

I don't want to eat. Two steps up, sometimes one step back.

I think about her (him) all the time. Look at my new friends.

He (she) better be hurting too! I'm beginning to like myself again.

Damn the S.O.B.! It's great to be alive!

I'm renewed!

Some of Jot's friends see a mean Giant Dragon with fangs who's breathing fire at the top of the slide. The dragon frightens them right past the slide. Instead, they bury their heads, and imagine they read on the Dragon's T-shirt such things as: "Don't go down the slide — you must control your emotions — don't cry or show weakness — you aren't strong enough to take any more pain — you may end up crazy!" They stay in this self-chosen hell until they somehow muster the courage to confront the Giant Dragon, only to discover that the sayings on the Dragon's T-shirt are only myths. At last Jot's friends risk the slide and they too discover the steps leading to the warm sunshine.

Are you like Jot? Do you see a Dragon? What do you see on the T-shirt? Are you willing to risk the *slide* into pain, in order to gain access to freedom?

This check mark offers a good overview of the divorce grief process, and illustrates many of our fears about grieving. An *intellectual* understanding of the grief process may help us to *emotionally* understand our feelings as well. Eventually, however, each of us must allow ourselves to *experience* grief, not just talk about it.

Let's see what we can learn from a head trip. As a beginning, a list of the grief symptoms commonly felt during divorce will help you see that your feelings are much like those of others.

Many people talk continuously about their situation until they drive away their friends, and they need to seek new ones (the "verbal diarrhea" stage). The grieving person needs to stop *talking* and begin *expressing* how he or she feels! (If you find — or friends tell you — that you continually repeat yourself, this is a likely indication of a need to *express* your feelings rather than talking about them.) Later in this chapter you'll find some help with this.

Grief has a *push-pull effect*. Having been hurt, you have a big, empty feeling in your gut; and you expect friends to help you fill it. You try to talk with friends and get close to them, but at the same time this empty feeling — like a big wound — is very vulnerable to being hurt again. When people get too close, you tend to push them away to prevent further emotional pain. Thus, you pull people toward you emotionally, but push them away when they get *too* close. Quite a mixed message for your friends!

With grief, *feeling emotionally drained* and *not sleeping* are frequent problems. Many people in grief have trouble falling asleep at night without using drugs or alcohol. Often they wake up very early in the morning, unable to go back to sleep yet too tired to get up. At a time when sleep is needed most, you have difficulty sleeping, and the hard emotional work has you tired all day long. Grief *is* hard work, and you will likely feel tired continuously until you have finished your grief process.

Eating is a problem during grief. You may have a feeling of tightness in your throat and find swallowing difficult. Sometimes your mouth will be very dry, also making eating difficult. You may not even have any appetite and may have to force yourself to eat! An empty feeling may occur in your stomach as though you were hungry, but you do not feel *hungry*. For these and other reasons, most people lose a great deal of body weight during grief. Although a few people do *gain* appetite and weight during grief, this is a small percentage compared to those who lose weight. During a break in one of my divorce seminars, several participants were comparing their loss of body weight during divorce grief. Of the six people present, all had lost at least 40 pounds! While the amount may not always be so dramatic, the unanimity is not surprising.

One of the most useful questions in the *Fisher Divorce Adjustment Scale* asks about *sighing* often. People are often not aware that they are sighing, but it is an indication to others that the person is grieving a great deal. Not only does the sigh itself release body tension, but also the deep breathing of the sigh seems to ''carry feelings from the gut'' that need release.

Rapid mood changes are typical during divorce grief. You have moved from the black pits of grief and finally feel good. Then, without apparent reason, you are out of control emotionally, unable to keep from crying. The whole sudden mood swing may have been triggered by conversation with a friend or acquaintance who said something to you or did something for you. You were feeling fine and in control until then. Your change to the depths of grief again leaves that person confused and sad, not understanding what he or she did to upset you. For your part, the downer is made even worse because you feel bad about *feeling* so out of control! The incident is a clear sign that *you have not completed your grief work yet!*

There may be a sense of *loss of reality*, of being in a daze, in an unreal world. You observe the environment as though watching a movie, remote and detached from the events happening around you. You are unable to wake up from this dream to the real world.

You may experience a period of *lack of contact with your emotions*. You are afraid to trust your feelings because of your inability to control them. The emotional pain is so great, you have to protect yourself from feeling too much by deadening your emotions. You may sense an emotional ''numbness.''

Many people experience quite a bit of *fantasizing* during grief. You may fantasize that you see the former love-partner, or that you hear his/her voice. You may fantasize that a part of your body is missing, as though your heart were removed, symbolizing the loss of the other person. This fantasizing may be frightening if you do not recognize it as part of grief.

Loneliness, lack of concentration, weakness and helplessness, depression, guilt, lack of interest in sex, and perhaps even the feeling of *impotence or frigidity* may accompany grief. *Self-criticism* — a need to continually question your errors and how you would relive the past differently — persists.

Anger is a part of grief that results from the apparent unfairness of the loss. Anger directed toward the former love-partner may approach rage in its intensity. We will look at it in detail in the next chapter.

Suicidal feelings are common during divorce grief. Approximately three-fourths of the participants in the divorce seminars admit to having experienced some suicidal thoughts during their grief periods. Research indicates a much higher than normal rate of actual suicides occurs among persons engaged in the divorce process.

All of these feelings can be overwhelming! Uncontrollable mood swings, loss of reality, fantasies, depression, suicidal feelings...one may wonder fearfully, "Am I going crazy?" For most people this is a difficult fear to discuss. And holding that fear inside makes it even scarier, even more crazy feeling. The "craziness" is a *real* feeling, but is related to the situation rather than to a permanent "psychological diagnosis!" You may well be experiencing a normal grief reaction if you feel you are going crazy.

These grief symptoms may be handled by acknowledging them, accepting that they indicate grief work to be done, allowing yourself to feel the pain without denial. Crying, shouting, and writhing are other nondestructive actions to express your grief. Make a decision to manage the grief by deciding on an appropriate time and place to do grief work. On the job, for example, is *not* the time to cry and grieve! At work you must put the grief aside — "on the shelf," so to speak — and concentrate on your job. Because you have set aside time to grieve, your emotions become easier to control at other times, and you do not become caught in the grieving. But be sure you *do* grieve during the time you have set aside for grieving! If you do not manage the grief, it will manage you!

If you do not do your grief work, your body may express the repressed feelings of grief in psychosomatic symptoms of illness. You may have simple ailments like headaches, or you may develop ulcerative colitis, arthritis, asthma, or ulcers. Unresolved grief puts a great deal of stress upon your body, and may increase your medical and hospital bills.

Often people are reluctant to take the divorce class because they do not want to experience the pain and crying of grief again. I have learned to translate this reluctance into their need to complete grief work. Somewhere deep inside, you will know when the grief work is completed because of the feeling of *letting go* that you experience. You cannot be pulled down into the grief pits again!

In this part of the climb it will be helpful to identify the five stages of grief. An intellectual overview will help us to work through the five stages emotionally. We are all greatly indebted to Dr. Elisabeth Kubler-Ross for her fine work in helping to clarify the stages of the grief process.

Stage 1. The first reaction to the sense of loss is *denial*: "This isn't happening to me. If I just wait a while, everything will be okay and my lover will come back." There is often a state of emotional shock, numbness, and denial of any feelings. One may enter into a robot-like phase, acting as though nothing is happening, repressing anger and becoming depressed. Best manners are extended toward the former love-partner, in the hope that it is all a bad dream and that person will not really *leave*! No one wants to tell friends and neighbors that our love-relationship is ending. Indeed, we don't want to tell *ourselves*!

Stage 2. As one gradually begins to accept the ending of a love-relationship a feeling of *anger* develops. The anger that has been turned inward, contributing to depression, is now turned toward others. Expressing the anger feels good, but there is also concern that the other person will not return *because* of the anger, thus some guilt and ambivalence. The frustrations that have existed in the relationship for years begin to come out. Friends may wonder how you have tolerated that person when you have been so emotionally upset in the love-relationship for so long. In turn, you may go to great lengths to convince others how terrible your former partner was, resulting in a "Catch-22" situation: you lose both ways. If you talk about how *good* that person is, how do you stay angry? But if you say how terrible that person is, then the question becomes why you chose to love such a terrible person in the first place! You have started working through the grief process when you admit and express the grief anger.

Stage 3. Beginning to face the fact that the love-relationship is ending, yet reluctant to really let go, one may start *bargaining*: "I'll do anything if you'll just come back. I'll change my ways, and put up with anything. Just take me back!" This stage is dangerous for the divorce process because many people *do* get back together, for the wrong reasons — to avoid the loneliness and unhappiness of ending the love-relationship. They are not choosing to live successfully with the former love-partner, but rather choosing the "lesser of two evils."

Stage 4. Stage four of grief is a final *letting go* of the love-relationship, and is, in a sense, the darkness before the dawn. Depression is typical during this stage, but the depression is different from that of stage one. This depression is a "blahs" feeling: "Is this all there is to life?" There is much internal dialogue about the meaning of life: "Why am I here on earth? What is the purpose of my life?" This is a stage of personal growth to build a stronger identity, to find a deeper purpose for living, and to make life more meaningful.

A number of people feel suicidal during this stage: "I've tried so long and worked so hard, and here I am down in the pits again. I don't want to let go!" Because the stage sometimes comes so long after the actual separation, people are surprised to feel so depressed again. It is discouraging to have worked so hard but feel so little progress. I have found that people who are aware of this stage get through it much easier. They are comforted to realize that there is a purpose for the depression they are feeling, that it will not last long, and that it is different from that of early-stage grief.

Stage 5. This is the stage of *acceptance* of the loss of the love-relationship. The person has begun to feel free from the emotional pain of grief and to feel no need to invest emotionally in the past relationship. Now one can begin to move on up the mountain toward fuller personal freedom and independence.

It is critically important to work through these five stages of grief before one enters into another love-relationship.

Children, too, must grieve an important loss, although sometimes it is difficult for us as parents to let them do the grieving they need to do. We see them starting to cry because they miss their noncustodial parent, and we want to take away that pain and reassure them, "Now don't cry, it's okay. Your father (mother) will be back. You will get to see him (her) in the future." Reassurance is not necessarily what kids need, rather they need some sort of acceptance: "You feel very sad to have your father missing. You feel very sad living away from your father whom you love so much." It is easy for us to get our own emotions and guilt involved instead of allowing the child to express his or her feelings and emotions. Children will tend to cry and grieve more naturally than adults, I think, until we take away the permission and start interfering with the process.

The same may be true with the anger part of grief. The child may be very angry about being separated from a parent and having a lifestyle change. When children start expressing their anger, adults often try to take that anger away by saying, "Well, you just need to grow up and understand. Someday you'll see that what we did was normal, natural, and healthy." *Allow* the children to just be angry; try saying, "You feel very angry toward your father for being gone."

Children will go through the five stages of grief described earlier. They will start out by denying that their parents are separated and believing the parents will get back together again. As they proceed through the stages of anger, bargaining, and so on, children need to be *allowed* to work through all five stages of grief. The exercises described above, plus the check list at the end of this chapter, can be very helpful for children as well as for their parents.

Obviously, there is a difference in the children's loss because parents do not divorce the children. The relationship between child and parent hopefully will persist, although in many cases the child does not see the noncustodial parent.

As with all other feelings, a parent who *shows* the child how to grieve is far more influential than the parent who *tells* children about grieving. Children will emulate a grieving parent, and will gain much from experiencing that healthy and needed release.

I hope you are helping your children of divorce to grieve, rather than hindering them by not giving permission or not showing them it is OK. Try to allow your children to work through the process described in this chapter.

There is a *process* of grief. Many people are afraid of grieving because it could show weakness, or maybe even signs of "going crazy." It is reassuring to find that other people experience many of the same feelings and symptoms of grief. We may emotionally work through the grief stages effectively, overcome our fear of grief, and feel safer in our grief work. This process gives us *permission* to grieve with a minimum of fear and anxiety.

Take time now to get out your handkerchief and see if you can let go of some more grief while you rest on the trail. Now that you understand the grieving process and have permission to grieve as a mentally healthy activity, you may feel freer to do some needed grieving (maybe including some past loss also). I suggest you call upon a trusted friend, family member, clergyperson, or counselor to provide support (without interference) while you allow yourself to express the depths of your grief.

In our seminars we have an important, experiential homework assignment that I think you would find helpful also. It is to write a letter of "goodbye" to one of the areas of grief mentioned earlier in the chapter. It may be goodbye to your home, to the relationship, or to a past loss.

The letter is intended to help you actually do the emotional grieving and letting go. It is a difficult assignment, so I suggest you start with one of the more superficial losses. Eventually, you can write a letter of goodbye to the major loss. The letter may or may not be mailed to another person. It is really for *your* benefit. In most cases, you will not want to share the letter with the person you are grieving about.

Below is an excerpt from a letter of goodbye that a woman in a recent divorce class wrote. It will give you insight into her thoughts and feelings, and maybe it will help stimulate you to write your own letter of goodbye. I urge you to read it thoughtfully, then begin work on your own letter(s).

goodbye

    goodbye to the New House that I spent endless afternoons and weekends looking for ~ making sure that it met all the rigid requirements. I'll probably never find another house like that again. It was so much more than a house~ it represented an end to looking, an achievement of a goal; a new beginning; a readiness for our family to begin. And now I'm back at the beginning of the beginning. So very far away from that place I'd worked so hard to get to. God, I was so tired of searching and so grateful to have found it, and now I've lost it all.

    goodbye to the home we were making for our future. goodbye to the tulips we planted in the Fall but that we never saw together in the Spring when it came time for them to bloom. goodbye to the plans we made for the nursery and fixing up the old cradle for the baby we never had.

    goodbye to all that potential our new beginning was bringing us.

    goodbye to the confidence and satisfaction I felt as "your mate" ~ the well-defined role; knowing what was expected of me.

    goodbye

    I've wanted so badly to say goodbye. To let go of you.
    To push you swiftly and completely from my life
        as you have done with me

    What is it that I'm holding onto?
        Promises
            the good old "as-soon-as-we" promises...
                degrees...
                travel...
                jobs...
                honeymoon...
                money...
            funny how they changed to "as-soon-as-I" promises

I loved you because you were the other half of a marriage that
        I needed very badly in order to feel whole
    because you were the future father of our family
    because I needed someone to care for, to nurture, to parent;
        you made me feel needed.

I guess I've already said goodbye in more ways than I would have thought possible. You've been gone for a year and a half. Somehow I'm still here; all here; and no where, not even on the final decree, does it say that I am now only half a person with only 50% of the purpose, of the value that I once had. I am not trying to say goodbye to my self-worth or dignity ~ I've not really lost that ~ but rather I am trying to say goodbye to my need for your credibility stamp on those feelings in order to make them valid.

The last goodbyes are the positive ones. For they are goodbyes to the negatives.
     goodbye to the feelings of enslavement
     goodbye to your picky little dislikes
         onions, mushrooms, olives and
         my flannel nightgown and
         getting up early and
         Joni Mitchell and
         my friend Alice and
         going to the zoo.
     goodbye to your lack of direction and
         your lack of creativity and
         your lack of appreciation and
         your lack of sensitivity
     goodbye to your indecisiveness and
         your stifled, dried-up emotions and
         your humorless sense of humor

     goodbye to feeling ashamed of getting angry and showing it,
         feeling embarrassed for being silly
         feeling guilty when I knew the answer and you did not.

                          goodbye
                          Trisch

Now, dry your eyes and read through the check list for grief work. As before, please be sure you have dealt thoroughly with this rebuilding block before you go on. Grief is a tough and painful stage. Do not just bury it! And do not try to get through it in the time it took you just to read this chapter. Use your lifeline friends (see chapter nine) for help as you work through your grief. The mountain will still be yours to climb when you are ready!

1. *I have given myself permission to grieve if I need to.*
2. *I am not burying the grief sadness but am trying to express it.*
3. *I now have physical and emotional energy from morning until night.*
4. *I have stopped feeling depressed most of the time.*
5. *I have no trouble concentrating.*
6. *I no longer feel like crying most of the time.*
7. *I have overcome the feeling that I am in a daze.*
8. *My emotions and moods are back in my control.*
9. *I have no trouble going to sleep and sleeping all night.*
10. *I rarely sigh now.*
11. *I notice my body weight has stabilized.*
12. *My appetite is good.*
13. *I no longer feel mechanical in my daily living habits.*
14. *I have outgrown the feeling that I am losing my mind.*
15. *I have stopped talking continuously about my crisis.*
16. *I have no thoughts of attempting suicide.*
17. *I have no more lump in my throat.*
18. *My stomach feels relaxed and at ease.*
19. *I am beginning to be emotionally close to people again.*
20. *I feel emotionally alive rather than emotionally dead.*
21. *I understand the grief process.*
22. *I have identified which of the five stages of grief I am in.*
23. *I have identified any past grief that I have not experienced and worked through.*
24. *I have identified what I need to grieve [person, relationship, future].*
25. *I am comfortable talking about my feelings of grief with a friend.*
26. *I have written a letter of goodbye to the loss I am experiencing now.*

ANGER: Damn the S.O.B.!

You will feel a powerful rage when your love-relationship ends. Feeling anger is a natural, healthy part of being human. But anger is different than aggression, which is a destructive form of expressing anger. It's not healthy to keep your anger inside, nor to express it aggressively. You can learn to express both your divorce anger and your "everyday" anger constructively.

chapter six

I don't know what came over me. I saw his car in the parking lot and I knew he had met his girl friend and left in her car. I went over and let the air out of all four tires. Then I went behind the building and waited until they returned so I could watch them find his car with the tires flat. I watched them trying to solve their problem and I felt so good. I've never done anything like that before in my life. Guess I didn't know how angry I could get.

Jean

We are approaching a point in the trail where we are in danger of being consumed by the fire of anger. The possibility of fire is great during the divorce process, and if we do not deal with it adequately, the fire of anger can spread to the other rebuilding blocks and keep us from making progress.

Divorce anger is the extreme rage, vindictiveness, and overpowering bitterness that we feel when our love-relationships are ending. It is a special kind of anger that we usually have not experienced before. Many of our married friends do not understand it unless they have ended a love-relationship.

You may try to keep this anger inside and not express it. As a result, you may become depressed, because one cause of depression is anger not expressed. It is typical for people during the early stages of divorce not to express their anger and to become depressed. The dumper does not express it because he/she feels so guilty, and the dumpee does not express it because he/she fears the other person will not come back. So both are "nice" for a while, except that they feel a lot of depression.

Anger is expressed in violent ways many times. Many people, given the opportunity while they are angriest, will commit an act of violence during the divorce process. We are lucky if we are able to restrain ourselves and find more suitable methods of expressing these feelings of rage and vindictiveness. We can find more constructive uses for anger than destroying ourselves with depression and psychosomatic problems (headaches, body tension, ulcers, and the like). Also, since the fires of anger can spread to other rebuilding blocks, if we can work our way through this block, we will have much less trouble handling other parts of the trail.

This rebuilding block fits rather naturally into three phases. The first phase is learning to accept that *it is okay and part of being human to feel angry*. There are many myths in our society that say that to be angry is to be weak, childish, destructive, and sacrilegious. (We are supposed to "turn the other cheek." But *Christ* became angry and drove the money changers out of the temple! Why can't *we* be angry like that?) We have learned that it is not permissible to feel angry. Now we have to relearn that it is okay. This may be easy to do intellectually, but it is much more difficult emotionally. The strong emotional reactions we have received from others when we became angry may make us very reluctant to accept those angry feelings now. Just remember there is a difference between that *feeling* of anger and the way we *act* to express it!

The second step, after acknowledging that we are human and can feel anger, is to learn as many positive ways of expressing anger as possible — ways that will not be destructive to ourselves or to those around us. We can do it with humor, physical exercise, and other ways that we will explore in this chapter.

One of the most destructive things that happens to many people during the divorce process is the use of children as a vehicle for expressing anger at the former spouse. We may make children into spies when they come back from visitation. She will not allow him to see the kids until he pays child support; he will not pay child support until she allows visitation. We forget about what is best for the children because we are so intent on *getting* that other person. Getting back through the kids is hitting below the belt. For the sake of the children, if for no other reason, we really need to learn constructive methods of expressing anger.

The third stage of anger is to learn *forgiveness*. Those of you in the first two stages may react emotionally with a big outburst now — "I will *never* forgive!" Well, it is not just forgiving the other person but it is also learning to forgive *yourself*. When we take it down to the final line, we are usually angry at ourselves. You are responsible for that anger because it is your feeling, not someone else's. Although projecting blame for anger onto someone else may be a part of the process — the part that allows us to get out the anger that has been causing depression — when you get further along, you must learn to take responsibility for that anger yourself.

There is a powerful anger item in the *Fisher Divorce Adjustment Scale*: "I blame my former love-partner for the ending of our love-relationship." People who have not yet dealt with their anger will answer "Yes" to that question. Those who have worked on their rebuilding enough to have dealt with the anger begin to realize that failure, blame, and responsibility are two-way streets. What happened was part of a complicated interaction that did not work, rather than the fault of one person.

Taking responsibility for our anger may take a long time for some of us. We need a great deal of maturity and strength to do that. It is so much easier to blame the other! So the stage of forgiveness is actually learning to forgive ourselves, and letting go of our anger.

Let us take a breather along the trail now, and have a closer look at anger. Have you thought about how appropriate it is to feel very angry when your love-relationship ends? "What," you may ask, "is appropriate anger?" Anger that is related to the present situation is appropriate. Harry is frustrated because someone ran into his new car (one of the participants in the seminar ran into her ex's new car when he came to pick up the son); Jan feels angry because someone has said something mean to hurt her; Sharon may become angry when she is unable to accomplish a simple task such as threading a needle. Appropriate anger is realistic for the situation; the feeling fits the event.

Aggressive anger does not fit the event. Bea is driving and the light turns red; she also turns red. A chance remark is made and Bart starts a fist fight. The *response* is out of proportion to the event. Often this person is bringing up past anger that was buried, sometimes way back in childhood.

What about childhood and its relationship to anger? We start our lives in the womb, truly the center of our own universe. All of our needs are met while we remain completely passive. The first big trauma is birth, when we are thrust into the "cold, cruel world." We suddenly have to start bawling and screaming to get fed and changed. During the process of maturing we become more and more responsible for meeting our own needs, often a frustrating experience. Thus maturity is reached, in part, through a process of frustration and anger.

If we are taught as children to freely express our angry feelings in constructive ways, we do not accumulate and sandbag anger. But if we are not allowed constructive ways of expressing anger (such as those I will describe later in this chapter), or if we grow up among very angry people who greatly increase our normal frustration to abnormal levels, we accumulate what might be called *childhood rage*.

Anger which thus accumulates in childhood becomes like layers around our gut, and any small event may trigger off inappropriate behavior. You will not have to think very long to imagine someone you know whose anger expression is always out of proportion. Look out for these people during the divorce process. They sometimes do violent things, like running over people with cars!

A few pages back I said it was appropriate to feel angry when your love-relationship ends. In fact, it is not only appropriate but it is beneficial and productive. "What?" you say, "Anger is beneficial?" Yes, because anger helps us to let go and become emotionally distant from the former love-partner. People who are unable to express anger will prolong the letting go process. They turn anger inward, experience a great deal of depression, stay stuck, and are unable to end the strong feelings they have for that former love-partner. Anger that is unexpressed disguises itself in many forms, often in physical symptoms such as headaches, ulcers, or skin rashes.

The next point contains both the "good news" and the "bad news." Because people who divorce usually had trouble expressing anger in their marriages, they have a great deal of anger stored up. When the divorce anger comes, that stored-up anger explodes; and thus we have both the appropriate anger of the present and the anger of the past. That is the bad news. The good news is that expressing divorce anger often frees the person to also express the stored-up anger.

Victor posed a question in the seminar, "Why do we have to go through a divorce to talk about the problems that occurred five or ten years ago?" The answer is because it took the divorce anger to get those buried problems out in the open.

Because this is such a common problem in marriages, divorces, and remarriages, one of the important topics in my *Relationships After Divorce* seminars is to help the participants learn to express anger constructively through the techniques of *fair fighting*. This is a group of positive ways of expressing anger with your love-partner first developed by psychotherapist George Bach. Many professionals who work extensively with couples have contributed to the technique.

One fair-fight tool is use of "I messages" — communications that allow you to get the angry feelings out of the way so that closeness, intimacy, and love may come into the relationship. "I" messages were first introduced as a part of the *Parent Effectiveness Training* programs of psychologist Thomas Gordon.

"I" messages start with the word "I," and place the responsibility for your feelings on you, rather than making the other person the source of your anger. "I" messages also help you identify what it is you are feeling, rather than covering up your feelings by blaming the other person. Maybe the most important part of an "I" message is that it communicates to someone else what you are feeling. Learning to use "I" messages will help you communicate with all of the loved ones around you — lovers, children, friends, relatives. I suggest you start practicing "I" messages as a way of improving your interactions with others, and as a way of expressing anger constructively. A simple example: instead of "*You make* me mad!" try "*I get so mad* when you....!"

I used to think that all a couple needed to do to make their love-relationship work was to learn to love and be loved. As I matured in my professionalism and my own personal growth, I learned that expressing anger constructively is probably equally important in making a love-relationship productive and keeping it clear of all the garbage that accumulates. (Another cause of divorce — how many is that now?) Anger left unexpressed will grow like a volcano until it erupts. Talking out anger is the relief valve that keeps the pressure cooker (marriage) from exploding. And talking out anger usually leads to intimacy and good sex. It is worth it!

Anger is like a fire that must be burned up into the ashes of forgiveness. If we are passive, it is like throwing more logs on the fire and we never get to the ashes of forgiveness. You may need to learn methods of direct — but not aggressive — assertiveness in order to get your divorce anger fire to go out.

Many people find logs blocking the trail in this section that keep them from learning about anger with its many positive uses. I have encountered these people in counseling and have learned the feelings behind these roadblocks. Theresa had been very abused as a child and had accumulated childhood rage. We were trying to help her express her anger and I asked her what would happen if she expressed it with me. Theresa was silent for a long while, and then admitted that she felt I would hurt her. The fear of retaliation keeps many of us from expressing anger.

Anthony came into my office with a "Buddha smile" on his face. His son was flunking out of school by doing nothing, and his daughter was running away. I have learned that the smiling Buddha face is a mask for anger. Anthony, a self-ordained minister, was unable to express his anger because he had an image to maintain: "ministers don't act angry." But his anger came out with his children through physical abuse. His children reacted with appropriate angry *feelings*, but their *behavior* was harmful and not constructive. The children needed to learn positive ways of expressing anger, but emotionally they were learning instead to abuse *their* future children.

It is clear that we often learn to *express* anger the same way our parents did. We may learn to express it in *passive* ways (non-assertive), aggressive or hostile ways, or direct-but-non-hostile (assertive) ways. Sometimes it is a reaction to our parents' anger that we learn. Jim saw his father throwing temper tantrums and acting childish, and he decided that he would never be like his father by acting childish around his children. So when he felt angry he became the stoic who put on the stone-face mask, like Anthony's "Buddha." His face would look like granite, but he would never admit that he was feeling angry.

Or poor Jeannette — she was the scapegoat in her family. Some families have an unhealthy interaction style, whereby they need someone to blame for everything that goes wrong. They find a scapeboat and dump all of the blame upon him/her. When I was a probation officer, some of these families came to me for help. It was a temptation at first to remove the scapegoat from the home for placement in a foster home. But as I became more experienced, I learned that if you remove the scapegoat there are two possible reactions: either the caseworker becomes the scapegoat, or another member of the family becomes the scapegoat. There will always be a scapegoat until the members of the family learn to take responsibility for their own feelings rather than projecting their unhappiness upon another.

A person who has been a scapegoat in his or her family (were you?) will have great difficulty expressing anger. Anger is appropriate because this type of situation leaves a person with a great deal of childhood rage. There is a scapegoat in almost every divorce seminar, because the scapegoat is prone to divorce. Scapegoats have to do a great deal of emotional relearning before they can overcome the feeling that they are so worthless that they do not have the right to be angry. Being the scapegoat is so destructive that one may need to seek professional counseling to escape this destructive role.

And, oh! We must not forget the martyr. Almost every class I have taught has had someone in it who was either a martyr or the victim of a martyr. Martyrs try to live through other persons. They completely sacrifice themselves to "helping" others. Martyrs will give to others, seemingly without limit, at great personal cost to themselves. The feeling behind martyrdom may well be genuine, but the giver does things whether he or she feels like giving or not. *There* is the deep, subtle process going on. The giver is not giving because he or she cares, but from the fear of losing the other person or because it is a way of interacting that the martyr learned at an early age. This giving, for what turn out to be selfish reasons when we look closely, will cause resentment in the other person. But the other person will find it very difficult to express this resentment and anger because the martyr's self-denying style generates a nurturing response.

The principle operating underneath this relationship is that martyrs do not have identities of their own. They try to find their identities through other people. Living through others is what makes the martyr relationship so destructive and harmful to both people. In chapter twelve you will find an exercise which may help clarify the martyr role.

How do you escape being a martyr if you are one yourself? Or how do you help another person to escape being a martyr? The martyr who does not have an identity of his or her own needs to work at finding that identity; to stop exclusively giving; to learn to accept from others as well; to feel good about himself or herself; to find an identity through relationships, activities, interests, goals; and to escape the martyr role.

Some of us have been on the receiving end of martyrdom, and we have learned so much guilt that we have difficulty expressing our anger. Quite possibly if you have been on the brunt end of the martyr relationship, you have already begun to express your anger toward that other person. But, many people who have been on the brunt end have kept their anger turned in and have become martyrs themselves to the people around them. In many cases, we learn how to be martyrs by living with a martyr parent.

For some of us, learning about martyrs may be an emotionally heavy situation. Trudy watched and learned about martyrs in the seminar one evening. She went home, did not sleep all night, and called a friend to talk to the next day because it overwhelmed her to see that she had been a martyr in her marriage and had controlled her husband by making him feel guilty. So find a friend or a therapist to talk to if you need to work through feeling guilty for being a martyr.

It can also be helpful to observe that anger may be a *secondary* feeling that is covering up and disguising another feeling, such as frustration, rejection, inferior feelings, hurt, or feeling unlovable. It can be difficult to get in touch with these feelings. Anger just seems to come more easily for many of us, even though we feel bad about it. It is important to work hard at finding out if there may be other feelings confused with your anger.

I have found it helpful in the seminars to have people list their pet peeves. What really gets you angry when someone pushes a button? Elaine, so angry about Steve's efforts to gain custody of the children in court, may be feeling doubts about her abilities to parent. Charles may be so angry about Marie leaving the marriage because he is re-experiencing feelings of rejection from the past when his mother died. What are some of your pet peeves? And what are some of the feelings underneath that push your buttons and make you angry? It is worth a break on the trail to think about it for a time.

Earlier I mentioned that dumpees tend to feel more anger than dumpers. That may be easier to understand if we look for other feelings underneath the anger. Consider, for example, the frustration of being out of control. Most of the power is in the hands of the dumpers. They hold the cards, and the dumpees have to take whatever hand is dealt. It is frustrating to feel out of control, and frustration can lead to anger.

How about rejection? Dumpees usually are still in love, and the people they love are suddenly saying they do not love them anymore. That is deep rejection and often leads to anger.

How about the future? The dumpee may have thought the future was all planned. Then suddenly he/she has to face being alone (and lonely), and has to develop a new life plan. This may be accompanied by fear of making it financially, which is difficult and frustrating. The dumpee feels afraid — often *really* afraid. Anger can seem to be a beautiful way to fight being afraid, and may be one way to get the adrenaline going to overcome the fear. Dumpees thus tend to feel more anger, and their scores on the *Fisher Divorce Adjustment Scale* tend to reflect that. Again, each person is an individual, and there are some dumpers who feel a great deal of anger because of their unique situations.

I would like at this point to discuss positive ways to express anger; ways that will not be harmful to you or to others.

Let me reemphasize the important difference between the special *divorce anger* you may feel about your dissolution, and your anger in connection with other life situations. First I'll present some methods for constructively expressing the divorce anger, then some ways for you to express your anger *whenever* it occurs in your relationships. Divorce anger needs to be *vented* and *released* in a nondestructive way. Anger in future relationships — friends, family, lovers, children — needs to be *expressed directly, firmly, honestly,* but in a constructive way to encourage communication and a deeper relationship.

Another point that I feel very strongly about: Our temptation and desires are to take our anger out on the former spouses directly. We want to call them up and hurt them, get back at them, be vindictive, and express our anger directly to them. I do not believe that this is helpful in most cases. When you throw a few logs on the divorce anger fire, your ex may throw a few logs back in retaliation. Pretty soon the fire is consuming both of you. I suggest that you express your anger in other ways, such as those suggested here, rather than taking it out on your former spouse. This recommendation to avoid direct anger expression applies only to this special case of anger at your ex. Usually, I encourage the direct approach.

There are a few couples who have learned to express anger to each other in their relationships and are able to continue to express this anger as they go through the divorce process. However, most of you were not able to express anger in your marriage. How do you expect to express it constructively now? Later in this chapter I will offer some tools for dealing more effectively with your anger in the future. For now, concentrate on releasing the *old* anger that has built up toward your ex!

Humor is a very effective way of getting rid of anger. Harriet was the comedian of one class. She would come to the group and say, "I don't know what to tell people when they ask me where my former spouse is. I don't want to tell them that he's off with another woman. So I finally decided that the next time a person asks me, I'll tell them that he croaked!" She laughs and the whole class laughs, and everybody has vented angry feelings through laughter. A sense of humor is always valuable in life, but it is especially valuable in getting rid of anger.

One of the most effective ways of expressing anger is to call a friend and say, "I need to talk about this anger that I'm feeling toward my former spouse. I know I may not make sense sometimes. I know that I may become very emotional. And I know that some of the things that I say may not be what I'm really feeling all of the time. But right now I'm feeling really angry, and I need you to listen to me talk about my anger." A life-line support friend who will help you through these times is one of your best tools for dealing with anger.

Many people who experience divorce anger are able to use fantasies to help get rid of it. Sandy was an expert at this. She would fantasize the following incident: "I would go to the garden store and buy a sack of hot lawn fertilizer. Then in the middle of the night I would go over to my ex's house and write obscene four-letter words with the fertilizer in front of his house. Then he would read them every time he had to mow his lawn all summer long!'' We have to keep remembering these are fantasies and that we should not act them out! If you do not have much self-control, possibly you should not use fantasies because you may tend to act on them, which is likely to be destructive in most cases.

Physical exercise of any sort is usually helpful. Physical games, jogging, house cleaning, beating on a rug, or anything like that is especially helpful. *Anger is a source of energy and the energy has to be used up.* Physical activity is a good way of using up that energy.

You can be more effective in getting rid of anger through physical exercise if you use other techniques along with it. For example, when you play a game of golf or tennis, you can fantasize that the ball is that person's head. In addition, if you can do some grunting and groaning, using your vocal cords along with physical exercise, that would be more effective. When you go jogging, with each step you can mentally picture his or her face on the ground in front of you, and you can add grunts and groans.

If you feel comfortable using cuss words, this can be an effective way of getting more anger out. Using your vocal cords provides a vehicle for getting your gut feelings to literally come out your throat and mouth and be expelled from your body. Try getting your feelings out by screaming. Many of us would not be comfortable screaming with people around, but maybe you can find a place to go and scream alone. Charlene was able to do this by driving her car to a private place. Then she could park for a while and do the screaming, crying, and yelling that she found so helpful to get out her anger. Her kids became aware of it and when Mother was getting upset they would say, ''Mom's about ready to go to her screaming place again!''

Tears are another good way for some people to express anger. Crying is a positive, honest expression of feelings. Many people, especially males, have difficulty crying. You need to ''give yourself permission to cry'' — it will help you feel better. Crying is a natural body function for expressing sadness or anger.

Another effective way of getting rid of anger is to write a letter saying all of the things that you would like to say to that former lover. Write it in really big letters; maybe use a piece of crayon and write it with lots of anger. But after you have written the letter, do not mail it. Instead, take the letter to the fireplace and burn it up. You have both expressed and symbolically burned up your anger.

You can use the "empty chair," an effective Gestalt therapy technique. Imagine that the person sitting in a vacant chair is your former love-partner, and say everything that you would like to say to that person. If you are good enough at imagining, you can even switch chairs and say the things that person would say back to you. Then go back to your chair and say the things that you would like to say again.

Another simple and effective way of getting anger out is to take an old garden hose and cut off a three-foot piece. Careful now! Use this piece of hose only to beat on something that will not be damaged by it. The accompanying loud "smacks" add to the satisfaction of the pounding. (Please remember that such a device is *only* for nondestructive noisy release. Do not hurt yourself or anyone else!)

So you see there are many ways for you to vent your divorce anger. You will not find all of these ways helpful to you — in fact, you may have a great deal of resistance to some and be completely unable to use them. But you are only limited by your own creativity, ingenuity, and inhibition in finding ways for anger expression.

Incidentally, some people will not be able to express anger because of a need to *keep* it. It is like a companion. If you let go of that anger, you will not have it as a tool for punishing the other person. So you may have some sort of payoff or reward for keeping the anger. The question for you to think about is: What kind of person would you like to be? Do you like being an angry person, or would you like to let go of the anger?

Anger is one of the most important rebuilding blocks because it spreads to the feelings in the other rebuilding blocks. If the fires are burning out of control in you, then you will have trouble working up the trail until you get them under control.

A great sense of relief will result from working through your anger until there is nothing but ashes left. It will free you to have energy for other areas in your life. You can forgive yourself and the other person for the love-relationship not working out. You have stopped blaming yourself; you have stopped feeling like a failure;

you have found the internal peace that comes from letting go of everything that was painful. You find that you can talk to the former love-partner in a calm and rational manner without becoming emotionally upset. Now you can deal with friends — either your partner's or yours — without becoming irritated. You suddenly wake up and find there is sunshine in your life instead of the stormy cloud of anger. You realize that things just happened the way they happened, and that there is no point in blaming somebody.

Zack, a fellow in the divorce class, picked up a slogan that is very useful when you work through the divorce process: "It just doesn't matter." So many things that seemed important to us before just are not anymore. Once you have reached the stage of forgiveness, you no longer need to punish or be vindictive toward the other person.

I hope the preceding material has helped you learn to express your divorce anger. Now, I am going to discuss everyday, "garden variety" anger — the kind we all experience in response to the ups and downs of daily life.

First, notice that how we *act* (our behavior) is not the same as how we *feel* (our emotions). Feelings and behavior are really two different parts of who we are.

Anger is a *feeling*. Assertion and aggression are types of *behavior*.

Remember Jean at the beginning of this chapter? She is the one who let the air out of her ex's tires. Jean was feeling such strong anger that her behavior was definitely aggressive. It would have been possible for her to express her anger in other ways as well. For instance, she could have been even more aggressive and acted in some violent way toward her ex himself — maybe by physically attacking him. Or she could have taken an assertive approach to expressing her anger by confronting him directly and telling him exactly how she felt: "I'm so mad at you I feel like letting the air out of your tires! You've been unfair and unreasonable...!" Of course, that is the special situation I have advised against, but you get the idea: angry *feelings* can be expressed in different *behaviors*.

Put yourself in the following situations:

> You have been waiting in line for concert tickets for two hours. Two "friends" of the man in front of you walk up and say, "Hey, Joe, how about letting us in here?"

The child support check is two weeks late, and you really need the money to buy clothes for the kids before school starts next week. When you call your ex, the answer is, "Well, I had a lot of expenses from my trip to Hawaii, and I won't be able to pay you until next month."

You read in the newspaper that your state legislature has just voted itself a 20 percent raise — and voted to cut support for education by 10 percent.

Angry? Well, you should be! These situations and a thousand other examples of unfairness, abuse, thoughtlessness, and other mistreatment are good cause for anger. Never mind what you were told as a child — anger is natural, normal, healthy, and human! We all feel it at times. (If you think you *never* get angry, maybe you have already forgotten the difference between feelings and behavior. Go back and reread the paragraphs above!)

The question now is, "What do I *do* about my anger?" We have already discussed some ideas for releasing the strong feelings of divorce anger — humor, fantasies, exercise, screaming, crying, and others. These ways are helpful while you are getting rid of that powerful anger toward your former partner. But they do not give you much help for dealing with your anger in everyday situations because they are designed to release pent up anger in a situation you are no longer in. We need methods to use in situations involving on-going relationships.

Psychologists Bob Alberti and Michael Emmons, who wrote the first book on assertiveness training, *Your Perfect Right*, offer us a system for learning to let out angry feelings toward another person in positive, constructive, assertive (not aggressive) ways. I agree with most of what they have to say, and encourage you to try it in your own life. Like all the changes we have discussed in this book, it will take some effort, but you will find your relationships — and your own well-being — will benefit! The following excerpt from *Your Perfect Right* deals with anger: [2]

Our view of a healthy approach to dealing with anger is this:
(1) Recognize and allow yourself to believe that anger is a

natural, normal, healthy, non-evil human feeling.
Everyone feels it, we just don't all *express* it. You
needn't fear your anger.

(2) Remember *you* are responsible for your own feelings.
You got angry at what happened; the other person
didn't "make" you angry.

(3) Remember that anger and aggression *are not the same
thing!* Anger can be expressed assertively.

(4) Get to know yourself, so you recognize those events and
behaviors which trigger your anger. As some say, "find
your own buttons, so you'll know when they're pushed!"

(5) Learn to relax. If you have developed the skill of relax-
ing yourself, learn to apply this response when your
anger is triggered.

(6) Develop assertive methods for expressing your anger,
following the principles described in this book: be
spontaneous; don't wait and let it build up resentment;
state it directly; avoid sarcasm and innuendo; use honest, expressive language; avoid name-calling, put-
downs, and physical attacks.

(7) Keep your life clear! Deal with issues when they arise,
when you feel the feelings — not after hours/days/
weeks of "stewing" about it....

Go ahead! Get angry! But develop a positive, assertive
style for expressing it. You, and those around you, will appreciate it.

Before I end this chapter, a brief word is in order about the *religious beliefs* that prevent many people from showing anger. Many
believe that we should "turn the other cheek," and that expressing
anger is somewhat "sinful." I personally believe that expressing
anger in a positive manner and freeing myself from that anger is the
most spiritual thing I can do. I do not believe that God wants us to be
controlled by anger any more than by any other strong emotion.

Children of divorce experience the same type of extreme divorce
anger that parents do. I remember the daughter of one divorced
parent who became uncontrollably angry at her father in the swim-

ming pool one day. The anger was far stronger than the situation warranted, and was apparently a direct result of a feeling of abandonment, for which she blamed her father.

It is very easy for divorced parents not to allow their children to be angry. The custodial mother will many times try to establish a good relationship between her children and their father, even though he has not kept visitation appointments and appears to be involved in something other than the children much of the time. The mother may try to help the children to accept their father without being angry. But it is appropriate for children to be angry at the noncustodial parent who lets them down.

It is also easy for us to withdraw love when our children express anger. We may be so emotionally uptight ourselves that when children get angry, we immediately become unaccepting: ''Go to your room until you can learn to behave properly!'' We need to find that extra energy to listen to and accept our children's anger. But we also need to see that they do not become aggressive, have temper tantrums, or break things. Allow the children to express their anger in the same positive, constructive ways explained in this chapter. When they say that they are very angry at their father (mother) for not coming, just accept that and say, ''I think it's right for you to feel angry in this situation.''

Most of us learned our emotional blocks for expressing anger through some interaction with our parents. We were punished for being angry, or we were not allowed to be angry, or we were sent to our rooms and had feelings of rejection and loss of love. It is far better for children to learn that anger is part of being human and that it is okay to express anger in a positive way.

Do not stop climbing when you feel the fires of anger starting within you. This chapter should give you permission to feel angry, give you ways of expressing anger positively and constructively, and allow you to have nothing left but ashes. The fire may smoulder for a long time, but it is better to let it burn out so that you can be free. Take your time in this part of the trail, with forest fires raging around you, and be careful. It is important that you get through without destroying the people in your environment or destroying yourself. Uncontrolled anger can be very destructive.

My research indicates that the average person going through the divorce process stays angry at their ex-spouse for three years. How long will you choose to be angry at your former partner?

Check yourself with these statements before you go on. Remember to be honest with yourself!

1. *I can communicate with my former love-partner in a calm and rational manner.*
2. *I am comfortable seeing and talking to my former love-partner.*
3. *I no longer feel like unloading my feelings of anger and hurt on my former love-partner.*
4. *I have stopped hoping that my former love-partner is feeling as much emotional pain as I am.*
5. *I no longer feel so angry at my former love-partner.*
6. *It is not important any more that my family, friends, and associates be on my side rather than on my former love-partner's side.*
7. *I have outgrown the need to get even with my former love-partner for hurting me.*
8. *I no longer blame my former love-partner for the failure of our love-relationship.*
9. *I have stopped trying to hurt my former love-partner by letting him/her know how much I hurt emotionally.*
10. *I have overcome my anger and have begun to accept the things my former love-partner has been doing.*
11. *I am expressing my anger in a positive manner that is not destructive to me or to those around me.*
12. *I am able to admit it when I feel angry rather than denying my angry feelings.*
13. *I understand the emotional blocks that have kept me from expressing anger in a positive manner.*
14. *I am able to express my anger constructively rather than venting it inappropriately.*
15. *I am reaching a stage of forgiveness rather than remaining angry.*

LETTING GO of the Emotional Corpse

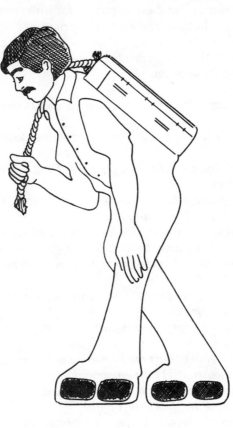

You need to stop investing emotionally in your dead love-relationship. It is easier to let go if your own life-bucket is full rather than empty. Dumpers tend to let go more quickly, often because they have let go even before they left. Failure to let go may be a symptom that you are not facing some painful feelings within yourself.

chapter seven

Stella: *"Harry left me four years ago and he immediately remarried."*
Counselor: *"I notice you are still wearing a wedding ring."*
Stella: *"Yes, It's very important to me."*
Counselor: *"And you wrote me a check for the therapy with Harry's name still on the bank account!"*
Stella: *"I guess I just can't let go."*

Some days I get a song in my brain that I keep humming over and over. How many songs can you think of that have to do with letting go? Here are a few to get you started:

Whatcha Going to Do When She Says Goodbye?
Breaking Up Is Hard To Do
One Less Bell To Answer
I Will Survive
I'm Gonna Wash That Man Right Outta My Hair!
I'll be Loving You, Always [for us old-timers]

I have had surprising difficulty finding information of any importance concerning how to let go. Yet most of us have ended a love-relationship at one time or another in our lives, even if it was when we were teenagers and dating. It is interesting that this common phenomenon has been researched so little. We have to depend upon the poets and song writers to teach us about ending a love-relationship.

First we need a definition of just what *letting go* is. Imagine your hands clasped together with the fingers intertwined, and then imagine pulling those hands apart while you continue to clasp. That gives you a graphic description of what I'm talking about. It involves the painful letting go of all the strong emotional feelings for that other person.

The feeling of being in love is not the only thing that is hard to give up. There are also anger, bitterness and feelings of vindictiveness. Whenever a person still talks about the former love-partner a great deal, whether in endearing or angry terms, I know that person has not let go of strong feelings for the ex.

It is common for people to claim that they want to continue being friends during the "honeymoon period" of the divorce process. Then when the dumper guilt and dumpee anger set in, the desire to stay friends begins to disappear. But many people strive so hard to remain friends that they fail to let go — and fail to allow the anger to come and *help* them do it. As a result, I find it advisable *not* to maintain the friendship during that early stage; wait until after you have let go. Trying to be friends may prolong the process and even endanger the possibility of being friends later on.

Another aspect that needs to be mentioned is the *runaway syndrome*. Most divorced people at some time in the process have a strong urge to run away. They want to get into a new community, away from where the former spouse is living. This will avoid the pain of running into the former spouse or his/her friends. Corinne had been married to a college professor who left her when he became involved with a young student. Driving her car down the street, Corinne saw him in his car with the younger woman. Before she could stop her car, she vomited. It is very painful to see that former love-partner with a new mate.

If you are running *toward* something, such as a new job, a former home with a support system of family or friends, or anything that is an advancement in your life, then maybe the move is advisable. If you are running *away* from dealing with the unpleasant situation, then you should reconsider. You are already under a stressful situation, and a major move will only add to the stress.

There may be advantages to staying in the present community and dealing with the painful feelings of seeing your former spouse and his or her friends. ("So you were married to the president of the Chamber of Commerce? I know him well.") People who move may just be burying and denying the process of letting go. Those who stay will likely be able to see and talk with the former spouse sooner without becoming emotionally upset. They will have dealt with this rebuilding block more effectively by confronting it.

There appears to be a connection between three key rebuilding blocks: *denying* that the love-relationship is ending; *grieving* the loss; and *letting go* of the dead relationship. As we climb the trail, we may be working on all three interconnected blocks at the same time.

(I want to talk to you dumpers for a moment; you dumpees may listen in if you want, because we will be talking about you.)

The dumper may want to "be kind" to the dumpee to avoid feeling guilty, but this only prolongs the process. If you are going to be a dumper, do it with strength, courage, and firmness. It is far kinder than being timid about dumping. Richard thought he would be a kind dumper, and made it a point to take Barbara (the dumpee) out to dinner every week, supposedly to make her feel better. But each time he did it, it was like throwing a few crumbs to a hungry cat. It kept the cat from finding other places to eat, and it kept the cat at a starvation level. Barbara failed to let go as long as there seemed to be some hope of reconciliation. Bluntness may be far kinder than "kindness" to the dumpee. Richard was being "kind" only to himself — easing his guilt feelings.

There are other situations that prolong letting go. Lengthy court hearings will drag things out. Children and pets that have to be exchanged at regular intervals may prolong the process, as may living close to each other. A joint business that forces you to keep dealing with each other is another delaying factor.

Another problem in letting go has to do with in-law relationships. Divorce usually includes separation from the ex-partner's family as well. While in most cases the ties with in-laws are broken or much loosened at the time of divorce, the breakup may have the opposite effect. In some situations, the in-laws' emotional ties remain closer to their son- or daughter-in-law than to their own son or daughter.

The Colorado State Supreme Court recently ruled that grandparents have visitation rights with their grandchildren regardless of who has custody. This landmark ruling will likely establish both a legal precedent and a custom which will result in maintaining the bonds of one's "family by a former marriage."

With or without all of these complications, the big question remains — HOW do you let go? For many of us, "How do I stop loving that person?" is the tough issue. It is much easier to let go, of course, if you have other things going for you. A good job, a good support system, friends and relatives who are helpful and supportive, some sort of internal fullness rather than emptiness — all of these will help fill the void created when the beloved person is removed.

There are some specific things you can do to help yourself let go. You can go through the house and remove all of those things that tend to keep you thinking about the former love-partner. Pictures, wedding gifts, birthday gifts, and similar mementos can be removed so that they are not a constant reminder. You may need to rearrange the furniture in the house, perhaps even to make the house look as different as possible from the way it was when you were living there as a married couple. The marriage bed is often an especially important symbol. You may need to put the bed in another room or sell it, or at least move it to a new spot in the bedroom.

You may want to make a collection of all those reminders of your former love-relationship and store them in a box in the garage or basement. Some weekend you may choose to do some *implosive grieving,* whereby you bring out all of these mementos and set aside a period of time to grieve as heavily as possible. This heavy grief period will probably be very depressing, and I suggest you have another person around for support. Becoming as much out of control as possible in your grieving may help you to let go more rapidly. By increasing the intensity of the grief, this *implosive grieving* may shorten the number of weeks or months it takes you to let go fully.

You also can make a decision to control your thinking and fantasizing about the former love-partner. Whenever you find yourself weeping about that person, think about something painful or something unpleasant in the love-relationship. That will lead you to stop thinking about the person. As an alternative, you may simply choose another image or subject to concentrate on, instead of focusing on the past love.

There is a more abstract answer to the problem of letting go. Often a pattern of behavior has at its core a specific feeling — such as fear of rejection, guilt, fear that one is not lovable, or low self-worth and lack of confidence. It is surprising how often we set up our lives to feel the feeling we are most afraid of! If we fear rejection, we either consciously or unconsciously set it up to be rejected. If we have a *need* to feel guilty, we set up situations that make us feel guilty.

When Teresa and Patrick came to see me for marriage counseling, his pattern of behavior was to seek rejection, and hers was to feel guilty. Their neurotic needs fit together perfectly! They went through years of marriage with her feeling guilty because he felt rejected. She set up reasons to feel guilty, thus feeding his feelings of rejection.

When love-relationships end, we tend to respond with the feeling which is at the root of our behavior. If it is rejection, we feel rejected; if guilt, we feel that. Unfortunately, such a feeling may be so great that one is not strong enough to endure it and let go at the same time.

If you are having a difficult time letting go, ask yourself, "What feeling would I feel the strongest if I did let go of my ex-love?" Maybe your reluctance to let go is actually covering up your inability to face the primary feeling that is underneath. For instance, you may be afraid to let go because it will force you to deal directly with your feelings of rejection. So, you avoid feeling rejected by not letting go. You will probably have to face that feeling directly before you will be able to let go. Get help from a life-line friend or a counselor if you feel the need for support.

Another area that is a problem for many people is dealing with all the phone calls, letters, and visits from the former love-partner. If it is evident that he or she is hanging on, you may feel irritated. But the fact that *you* keep allowing it to happen may indicate that *you* have not let go either! It takes two to keep this game going. If you simply refuse to play the game, it will be easier on everyone in the long run. You will have to become assertive, or perhaps even to start hanging up the phone or returning letters unanswered and unopened.

The goal of working through this rebuilding block is to emotionally invest in *your own personal growth* instead of investing in the dead relationship. There is no return on the investment in the relationship's emotional corpse. In contrast, the greatest possible return comes from investment in yourself.

Children of divorce deal with letting go by letting go of the old concept of the two-parent family. Suddenly it is a one-parent family, with a custodial and a noncustodial parent. Even if there is joint custody, the children still have to deal with different lifestyles. It is hoped that the children will not have to let go of a quality relationship with both parents.

The child may have difficulty, however, in dealing with the parents' ability to let go or not. This may become an important rebuilding block for children if they continually hear from one parent about all of the good things (or bad things) the other parent is doing. If the parents have not let go of the relationship, the children will tend to get caught in either the positive or negative feelings between the parents. This will prolong the adjustment process for the children.

Take time on the trail now to stand still and shake off those feelings from the past that keep you investing in the dead relationship. Jump up and down to feel strong inside, shake off the heavy burden you have been carrying, and find the free feeling that comes from not carrying that dead love-relationship on your back.

Finally, check yourself out on the items listed below. Have you really let go?

1. *I think of my former love-partner only occasionally now.*
2. *I rarely fantasize about being with my former love-partner.*
3. *I no longer become emotionally upset when I think about my former love-partner.*
4. *I have stopped trying to please my former love-partner.*
5. *I have accepted that my former love-partner and I will not get back together.*
6. *I have stopped finding excuses to talk to my former love-partner.*
7. *I rarely talk about my former love-partner with friends.*
8. *I have outgrown any feelings of romantic love for my former love-partner.*
9. *I no longer wish to continue a sexual relationship with my former love-partner.*
10. *I have given up my emotional commitment to my former love-partner.*

11. *I can accept my former love-partner having a love-relationship with another person.*
12. *I feel like a single person rather than a person in a committed love-relationship with my former love-partner.*
13. *I am no longer angry at my former love-partner.*

SELF-CONCEPT:
Maybe I'm Not So Worthless After All!

It is okay to feel good about yourself. You can learn to feel better about yourself, and thus gain strength to help you adjust better to a crisis. As you successfully adjust to a crisis, you will feel even better about yourself! If you are experiencing a personal identity/rebellion crisis, you may be seriously straining your love-relationship.

chapter eight

When I was a child, my father continually warned me about getting a
"big head" and becoming "stuck on myself." Then I went to church and
learned that I had been born sinful. At school it was the jocks and the brains
that got all the attention. Finally I married so there would be someone who
thought I was worthwhile. It made me feel good that someone cared. But
then she became a pro at pointing out my faults. I finally reached a point
where I began to believe I was truly worthless. It was then that I decided to
leave the marriage.

Carl

Wow! This self-concept portion of the trail is crowded with people who appear unable to continue the climb. Some sit on rocks, dejected, without energy left to climb. Some are lying on the ground
like door mats, expecting everyone to walk on them. The faces of
some show the effects of criticism and feelings of worthlessness.
Some seem almost invisible as if a shield surrounds them, blending
them into the background.

Notice those people who are followed everywhere by a black
cloud! Rain falls on them, but not on those around them. That woman over there seems to have misplaced her black cloud for a while.
She is anxiously peering over her shoulder, stumbling over rocks —
can she be searching for the lost cloud? Sure enough, the cloud has
caught up with her and is raining on her again, and she actually
seems more content now.

In this portion of the climb, learning more about self-concept and
ways to improve it are the main concerns. Self-concept is the skele-
ton that supports personality. When the self-concept becomes fractured, the whole personality begins to fragment.

When I was growing up I thought I alone suffered from an affliction called "inferiority complex." I never realized that the term was
used so often because many others were feeling inferior also! I have
often asked the participants in seminars to raise their hands if they
want to improve their self-concepts — usually *all* hands go up! Do
you see how important this rebuilding block is?

Have you ever wondered whether self-concept exists at birth or if
it is learned later? Apparently we learn much of how we feel about

ourselves at an early age from the significant people around us, including parents and siblings, teachers, ministers, and relatives. This basic level of self-concept is later influenced strongly by peers — especially during the teen years. As an adult, the love-partner becomes a primary source of validation and feedback, and greatly affects one's feelings of self-worth.

Many marriages that end in divorce developed a pattern of inter-action destructive to the self-concept of the parties involved. In fact, some become so destructive that the parties may not be able to end the marriage due to feelings of worthlessness. For example, the bat-tered wife often thinks that she *deserves* the emotional and physical battering. She is unable to leave the marriage because she would not be able to make it on her own. Many people have suffered an erosion of their self-concept in bad marriages before seeking relief in divorce.

But when the physical separation comes and the love-relationship ends, self-concept hits an all time low. So much of a person's identity is involved in the love-relationship that when the marriage fails, the identity suffers. I administered the *Tennessee Self-Con-cept Scale* (a paper-and-pencil psychological test designed to meas-ure feelings of self-worth) to recently separated people. It would be hard to find another group of people whose average score was as low as theirs. Ending a love-relationship can be devastating to self-con-cept. In fact, feelings of self-worth at this time may be the lowest ever experienced. A low self-concept immobilizes some people emo-tionally, making them unable to function in their jobs, in their par-enting of children, or in their interaction with others.

Further study of the self-concept scores of this same group of people showed that people with a good self-concept were better able to adjust to the ending of their love-relationship. The research con-firms what our common sense tells us: a good self-concept makes adjustment to a life crisis easier.

Obviously feelings of self-worth are very important to the way we live. Since ending a love-relationship is usually detrimental to self-concept, most of us need to improve our feelings about our-selves after experiencing a major life crisis such as this. It is reas-suring to know that self-concept can be enhanced. That is an excit-ing and optimistic viewpoint — we can relearn, grow, and change! We do not have to be saddled with old feelings of low self-worth.

In the divorce and personal growth seminars which I have taught continuously since 1974, changes in self-worth are among the most significant outcomes for participants during the 10 weeks. What techniques are used? How do people make such big changes? Let me share with you some tools you may use to improve your self-concept.

Step one seems obvious, but is often overlooked. You must *make a decision to change.* A few years ago, I discovered several clients who were being followed by little black clouds — like those people we met earlier on the trail. When there was progress in therapy, they would become uncomfortable, look for the cloud, and expect rain to fall!

Frustrated, I decided to take a solitary walk in the mountains. I hiked up the Big Thompson Canyon in the Rocky Mountains. Near the top of the trail is a little sign pointing out a Douglas fir tree uprooted by the wind. The tree had been lying on the ground long enough for the end of the trunk to bend around and continue growing toward the sunlight. The new growth was pointing toward the sky for about 20 feet. Because the old trunk's roots stick mostly out of the ground, one wonders how the tree could grow for so many years! Besides the trunk, several branches also reach from the upper side of the trunk to the sky. One of these branches is about 30 feet high.

I thought to myself, as I studied this tree, that it was uprooted in its life just as a person's life is uprooted by a crisis such as a divorce. The tree sought its own fullest potential, continuing to grow and reach for the sky. I was greatly moved by the sight of this tree. I realized that there is a force within each of us that will help us to reach our full potential after a crisis has uprooted our lives. The tree's continuing reach for the sky led me to develop my belief in changing self-concept.

We need to find and listen to that inner source of emotional energy which encourages the development of our potential. If we get in touch with that source — whether it be called a religious soul, a psychological ego, or the life force — we will be capable of making the changes that we desire. I suggest that you look within yourself for this source of strength and use it to become the person you would like to be.

If you make a decision to improve your self-concept, almost everything in your life will be affected: your work; your relationships with other people; the way you parent your children; your choice of a partner in a future love-relationship; and, most of all, the way you feel about yourself. Enormous changes may occur in your personality and your life if you proceed to improve your self-concept. The decision is the first and perhaps the most difficult step. If your commitment is firm, the steps which follow will come much more easily.

Step two is to *change the way you look at yourself.* Most people can easily list 20 things they do not like about themselves. Why not make a list of 20 positive things you do like about yourself? When I give this assignment in my seminars, there are groans and comments such as, "How about two instead of 20?" I once received a phone call late at night from one of the participants. He started the call with, "Damn you! I came home from teaching school and started the list of things I like about myself. It took me an hour to come up with the first one. It took almost that long for the second one. Now it is 11 p.m. and I only have five things on my list!" That was the most important homework for him in the whole 10 weeks. This is an important task; take time to do it. Be sure to write the list down so you can do the next step.

Step three: *Say positive things about yourself aloud to others.*
Good things may be easier to write to ourselves than to say out loud.
All the old messages inside us start screaming, "Don't act stuck up
and conceited!" Ignore those messages; take your list and share the
comments with a friend. Get your courage up and break the
negative pattern. It is *okay* to make good comments about yourself.
It does take courage to say them out loud. Remember, changing
your self-concept is *not* easy!

Those voices that scream inside us are especially loud if a critical
person influenced us when we were growing up. In class Charlie
said that he could not do step two because his parents had told him
so often "not to get a big head." He was a good athlete in high
school, and the exercises could have helped him to build confidence
in himself. But the parent voices were louder, and he had learned to
be "humble." As an adult he could not say good things out loud
about himself because he still felt his parents would be unhappy!
That statement may sound ridiculous to you, but not to Charlie. He
was finally able to read his list aloud in the seminar, although with a
look of pain on his face. When he finished, everyone applauded; and
he said, "Boy, I feel good!"

Step four is a tough one: *re-examine your relationships with
others, and make changes which will help you* break destructive patterns and develop the "new you."

Much of your self-concept is validated by feedback that you get
from others. Take a hard look at your relationships. Which are constructive for your self-concept? Which are really more harm than
good? If you see that some of your relationships with other people
are destructive to your self-concept, choose either to end those relationships or to make them more productive and positive for *you.* Old
and established patterns of interaction are hard to change. Nevertheless, to remain in a comfortable relationship which reinforces a
poor self-concept is to *choose* to keep a major obstacle in your own
path of growth.

As a probation officer, I often heard people say that a certain juvenile in trouble "only needed to find a new peer group" to solve all
the problems. I found that, for juveniles, it is generally necessary to
make changes in both their peer group and their feelings about

themselves. They tend to seek feedback from others that basically agrees with their own self-concept. Peer group relationships powerfully reinforce the *present* level of self-concept. This happens partly because the group was chosen as a reflection of the self-concept: "I really feel at home with these people."

Changing your relationships may be very difficult due to your tendency to follow the old patterns and find relationships that reinforce your *present* level of self-concept. But I believe that if you sincerely want to feel better about yourself, you will need to invest in positive relationships — those which help you feel good about being you!

Step five: *Get rid of the negative self-thoughts in your head.* We all hear messages playing in our heads — *parent tapes* in Transactional Analysis vocabulary. These parent tapes may have originated from parents or from teachers, ministers, or other significant adults: "Be careful and don't let this success *go to your head.* Remember that it is *sinful* to be conceited and selfish. You think you're *smart,* don't you?" Such messages are destructive, and prevent you from improving your self-concept. They were originally designed to discipline and control. Unfortunately, they turn out to be neither helpful nor productive to us.

As adults, we choose whether we want to continue to listen to those messages or not. Say your own tapes out loud and write them down. Think about whether they are appropriate. The transactional analysts suggest you take these messages from your *parent* or *child* ego state and analyze them with your *adult* ego state to see if they are rational and appropriate messages *at this time in your life.* Then rid yourself of those that prevent progress toward feeling better about yourself.

You may need to express these feelings of not being okay in a counseling session, with life-line friends, or perhaps in self-therapy. Write these messages down or tape record them. You need to somehow "carry out the emotional garbage of the past," so you can stop letting it control and burden you now. Allow yourself to air, ventilate, express, and verbalize those old *not okay* messages. Move them out of your path toward improving your self-concept.

Step six may sound like a silly activity, but it worked for Jane, a member of one divorce seminar. I suggest that you *write positive* *notes to yourself and pin them up around the house* in prominent places: on a mirror or on the refrigerator, for example. These notes might be compliments such as, ''You have a pretty smile.'' The notes could come from the list of 20 positive things that you like about yourself. Jane came to a weekend seminar and was like an emotional corpse. She had a great deal of difficulty paying attention, but somehow this exercise rang a bell for her. She reported the next week that she had written about 100 notes to herself, even placing one on the toilet! She became a different person, her self-concept improved almost miraculously! Writing notes to herself appeared to make the big difference. Such a dramatic change is rare, but shows the potential power of *active effort.*

Step seven: *Open yourself up to hearing positive comments* from others. People tend to hear only what they want to hear. If you have a low self-concept, you will hear only the negative comments that other people make. When somebody praises you, you deny it, ignore it, or rationalize it by saying, ''Oh, they're just saying that. They don't really mean it.'' Some people protect themselves from hearing anything positive because their basic self-concept says that those positive comments do not fit. The next time a person praises you or compliments you, try to let that compliment soak in, rather than defending yourself against hearing it. This may be hard for you to do. But it is very important to break your negative pattern of hearing. When you can *hear* positive comments, then you will feel better about yourself.

Step eight: *Make a specific change in your behavior.* Determine a part of your personality which you want to change. Maybe you would like to say ''hello'' to more people, or to be on time to work or school, or to stop putting off small jobs, like making your bed each morning. Decide to change that behavior every day this next week. Make the change *easy* so that you can accomplish it and feel successful. Do not set yourself up for failure by deciding to make an impossibly big change the first week. Perhaps you will want to mark a check on the calendar to reward yourself a little each day. At the end of the week you can look back and say, ''I accomplished it! I've changed something! I'm *different* in this particular area of my personality.'' After you have accomplished this first step, then during the following week take a second step — another small change —

and begin! If you do this for several weeks in a row, you will notice significant changes in your personality which will improve your self-concept.

Step nine is one of the most fun. *Give and get more hugs!* There has been almost a fear in our society about touching other persons to show affection, probably related to the undue emphasis upon sex and the Victorian attitudes toward sex. Many people are not aware of the difference between affectionate and sexual touching. Some are afraid that any touching will lead to sexual involvement. Many of us avoid touching and hugging altogether. Many other societies appear to have overcome this hang-up and are more comfortable with touching.

A warm and meaningful hug from a friend reinforces far more than spoken words can. A hug heals us and improves our self-concept more rapidly than any other methods. It frees us, warms us inside, improves our feelings of self-worth. "I am worthwhile enough to be hugged!" may be the warmest message we can hear. If you can overcome your fear of touching and even ask for a hug (if you are not getting enough), you will make a big step toward improving your regard for yourself — and you will enjoy the process!

Step ten suggests you *work hard at meaningful communication with another person.* Some of the most significant growth I was able to experience after my divorce was the growth I experienced while communicating with friends. Ask for and give honest feedback about each other. Say things that you never said to anyone before. Call it as you see it! Such a dialogue provides a mirror for you to see yourself as others see you.

Step eleven has to do with therapy. You may *choose to enter into a therapy relationship* in order to enhance your self-concept. It is a safe place to talk about anything you want to. Guidance from a professional may shorten the time it takes to change your self-concept. Therapy does not have the stigma that it once did because most therapy now is personal growth oriented, whereas in the past therapy usually meant "mental illness."

Finally, be aware that divorce can be very damaging to **children's** self-concept also. Suddenly life has been uprooted. They feel rejected, lonely, alienated, and perhaps guilty, questioning what they did wrong that contributed to their parents' divorce.

Children's adjustment to divorce may be complicated if they are also going through certain growth stages which are, of themselves, threatening to self-concept. As a prime example, there is some evidence that the junior high years are the most difficult years in growth and development for most children. I have listened to many adults talk about the painful difficulties of their junior high years. Puberty means dramatic changes in the body: height; weight; sexual characteristics; body hair; and voice. Suddenly identity — or who they *thought* they were — is also changing. They are experiencing new attitudes and feelings, such as attraction to the opposite sex. Relationships with peers have become much more impportant. This rapid period of change is a real strain upon a teenager's self-concept. So if youngsters are going through extreme changes in themselves at the time of their parents' divorce, the children's self-concepts are more likely to be affected.

The exercises in this chapter are helpful to share with your children. In fact, doing the exercises together is a good way to increase family communication. So I suggest that you parents of divorced children take these 11 steps toward improving your self-concept, and assist your children in following the same steps.

If you work diligently at these exercises, you may be able to make some of the same changes that participants in the seminar are able to make. All you have to lose is your poor view of yourself! Make this part of the trail an important part of your growth. This rebuilding block will probably affect more aspects of your total life than any of the others.

Here is your check list for this portion of the trail. Once again, allow yourself adequate *time* to deal with this important area. When you are comfortable with most of these items, you are probably ready to resume the climb. Take care!

1. *I am willing to work hard to improve my self-concept.*
2. *I want to improve my self-concept even though I understand that it will change many aspects of my life.*
3. *I like being the person I am.*
4. *I feel I am an attractive person.*
5. *I like my body.*

6. *I feel attractive and sexually desirable.*
7. *I feel confident most of the time.*
8. *I know and understand myself.*
9. *I feel good being a woman or a man.*
10. *I no longer feel like a failure because my love-relationship ended.*
11. *I feel capable of building deep and meaningful relationships.*
12. *I am the type of person I would like to have for a friend.*
13. *I am attempting to improve my self-concept by using the 11 steps listed in this chapter.*
14. *I feel what I have to say is important to others.*
15. *I feel I have an identity of my own.*
16. *I have hope and faith that I can improve my self-concept.*
17. *I am confident that I can solve the problems facing me.*
18. *I am confident that I can adjust to this crisis.*
19. *I can listen to criticism without becoming angry and defensive.*

FRIENDSHIPS:
Where Has Everybody Gone?

The support you receive from life-line friends is very important and can shorten the time it takes you to adjust to the crisis. Friends are more valuable to you than lovers right now. You can develop friends of both sexes without becoming romantically and sexually involved. Divorce is threatening to many married people, so your married friends may slip away from you.

chapter nine

Maria and I had lots of friends and family around all the time. Most week-ends we'd have a bar-b-que, or go over to her sister's place, or take a picnic with two or three other couples. Since we split up, none of those people ever call me or drop by. How come married people don't seem to want us around when we're single?

                                                        Jose

As we climb the mountain, notice the different ways people handle the problems of friendship. While going through the pain of separation, some people insist on walking alone. They tend to with-draw, and they feel uncomfortable being with anybody else. You will notice others who are continually clinging to each other, as though they cannot be alone for a single minute. Always walking arm in arm, they even plan ahead so that they have no part of the journey to walk by themselves. Note also how few people continue to have any communication with friends from the days of their love-relationship.

It appears that we have to find new friends as we journey up the path. On this stage of our climb, finding friends appears to be a very difficult problem.

Did you ever, when you were married, look at your divorced friends with envy and wish you could be part of all of those inter-esting activities they were into? That you could go to the exciting events that your spouse was reluctant to go to? Well, now you are free! What do you think about the "glamorous" single life now? For most of us, especially when we first separate, the single life is not glamorous — in fact it is downright lonely and scary.

It is lonely, in part, because we tend to lose the friends we had when we were married. There are four main reasons: *number one* is that when you are ending a love-relationship, *you suddenly become an eligible love-partner,* and a possible partner for one of the peo-ple in a marriage. Thus, whereas you were formerly invited to all the parties as a couple because you were *safe,* now you are a single person and a *threat.* Suddenly people are looking at you as eligible, and invitations to married friends' parties diminish accordingly.

When I became divorced, I was working in a situation in which I had considerable contact with a married woman. Three months after my separation, I walked by her desk and she said, "You're sure a lot more sexy now that you are separated and getting a divorce!" I told her, "I don't really believe I've changed very much, but I feel you are looking at me differently now. It makes me feel like an object rather than a person." Though flattered by her interest, I was uncomfortable as a potential threat to her marriage.

The *second reason* we tend to lose friends is that *a divorce is very polarizing.* Friends tend to support either the ex-husband or the ex-wife, rarely both. Thus, we tend to lose the friends who have sided with our former spouse.

I think the *third reason* is probably the most important: *the fear that "If it can happen to you, it can happen to me."* Your divorce is very threatening to many marriages around you, so married "friends" slip away. Although you may feel rejected, actually it is their problem, and a reflection on them rather than on you. It is likely true that the shakier your friends' marriage, the quicker they will leave you. So, instead of feeling rejected, understand that the divorce has caused them to feel very insecure about their marriage. They withdraw from the friendship because they fear divorce may be a contagious disease!

There is a *fourth aspect* of friendship which is important to understand while you are going through divorce. Married people are considered to be part of the mainstream, accepted, couple-oriented society that is the cornerstone of our way of life. Divorced people, however, become part of the *singles subculture* — a part of our society that is less acceptable to many. This singles subculture may be somewhat hidden and difficult to find, especially until you become a single person. To be pushed out of the acceptable mainstream culture into the "questionable" singles subculture is a difficult adjustment.

There is a different standard of mores and values in the singles subculture. People hang a little bit looser; they tend to be a little bit freer, sort of a large fraternity or sorority. At a singles gathering,

"I'm divorced" becomes a *valuable* conversation opener, rather than a turn-off. If, as is often the case, the other person is also divorced, suddenly you have something in common and you can start talking to each other. Because the standards and mores are different, formerly-coupled people are not quite sure how to behave in the singles subculture and their first reaction can be somewhat of an emotional shock. You think, "Somebody's changed the rules, and I don't know what the new rules are!"

As you begin to work at rebuilding your friendships, you will find a *three-stage process.* In the *first stage,* you are so hurt, lonely, and depressed that you avoid friends unless it is very safe to be with them. The *second stage* begins when you can at last take the risk of reaching out to people, even when the fear of rejection looms large. The *third stage* is becoming comfortable with people, finding out that you are *okay,* and beginning to enjoy people without fear of being rejected.

Recently divorced persons frequently ask: "How do I make friends after a divorce? Where can I find someone to date?" The problem is that many formerly married people are out looking *desperately* for another love-relationship, instead of enjoying the people around them. The goal should be to get to know people, and some of these new acquaintances may become special friends or even lovers.

Start with friendships first. You can meet new people wherever you go — the grocery stores; classes in tennis, ceramics, cooking, language, personal growth; community groups; the library; work; or just out walking the dog. If you are genuinely interested in the people with whom you come in contact, you are sending out *vibrations* that make people want to respond. But if you are coming across as lonely, desperate, and needy, people will not want to be around you.

The vibrations I am talking about include your body movements, the way you walk, the tone of your voice, your eye contact, your style of dress, and all the subtle ways you show how you are feeling. Experienced people in the singles subculture can often tell if you are single by your vibrations. Note that even if you do not *intend* to do so, you are sending out some sort of signals. Are you inviting others to get to know you?

When you are ready to make friends and feel comfortable doing so, then there are some specific steps you might want to take. The people who enroll in classes or groups such as my divorce and personal growth seminar have found one way to handle the rebuilding block of friendships. Participating in such a seminar may help you find deep and meaningful friendships you never thought possible. Check with local churches, colleges, Y's, mental health centers, marriage counselors, and psychologists. If you do not find such a seminar, you may want to start a group of your own with five to ten people of both sexes who are interested in reading this book and discussing the ideas. Meet in each others' homes. Have a time for work and a time for play; spend some time in group discussion and some time just socializing with each other. Share your common concerns and feelings. It may be advantageous to have people who do not know each other, so you will not get into old patterns of gossip. I found this kind of discussion group provided me with some of my most memorable and enjoyable evenings in my own divorce process.

There is a concept that I feel so strongly about that I want to write it in capital letters. I SUGGEST YOU DO NOT BECOME INVOLVED IN ANOTHER LONG-TERM, COMMITTED LOVE-RELATIONSHIP UNTIL YOU HAVE EMOTIONALLY WORKED THROUGH THE ENDING OF THE PAST LOVE-RELATIONSHIP! Becoming involved too soon results in carrying the emotional garbage from the past relationship into the next one. You would likely marry someone just like the one you left, or someone just the opposite. In either case, the chances of the same problems occurring in the next relationship are great.

A healthy process of divorce might be described as "learning to be a single person." Many people never learned to be independent individuals before they were married. They went directly from their parental home to the marriage home. If you have not learned to be a single person, it is easy for you to *hide* in another relationship. Because your emotional needs are great when you are ending the love-relationship, the comfort of another love-relationship is appealing. Nevertheless, there is truth in the paradox that when you are ready to face life alone, then you are ready for marriage.

But you do need friends, and relationships with potential love-partners based upon friendship. If you can build open, trusting, honest relationships with good communication and opportunities for both persons to experience personal growth, then you will probably work through the divorce process more rapidly.

Sometimes it is hard to tell whether a current relationship is limiting personal growth. The best criterion might be to ask, "Am I learning to be a single person?" If you feel you are losing your identity because of your love-relationship, then you probably need to back off from it. (This is easier said than done in many instances! But I stress again how important it is to GET YOURSELF TOGETHER first!)

Here is an exciting concept that you may learn for the first time: *It is possible to develop a close, nonsexual, nonromantic friendship with a member of the opposite sex!* This may be the way it happens for you: you tentatively make friends, but you are very cautious because of your fears of closeness and intimacy. The friendship becomes important, and you suddenly realize that you want very badly to maintain this friendship because it feels so good. You have a feeling down inside somewhere that if the quality of the friendship changes to a romantic, sexual one, it will be less meaningful, and it will become not so special anymore. Then you realize that you want to keep this *friendship* very much, and will go to great lengths to invest emotionally so that it will continue to grow. Such a friendship brings a free and exhilarating feeling. It also destroys the myth about *never* becoming a friend with a member of the opposite sex.

There was an old wives' tale about this kind of friendship destroying marriages, which you will now recognize as pretty phony logic. There are just as many kinds of friends as there are vegetables; and trying to make a tomato into a zucchini is difficult, if not impossible! You have learned something that will enrich your next marriage if you so choose. To have friends of both sexes is one indication of a healthy relationship.

While you are working to develop new friendships, you may also be hearing a barrage of negative comments about marriage in the singles subculture. There are people who rant and rave and shout from the hilltops that they will never get married again. They compile long lists of all the painful and negative aspects of marriage. And if there is someone who decides to remarry, they even send cards of *sympathy* to the couple! You need to realize that these people are as threatened by marriage as some people are threatened by divorce. Perhaps a bad marriage led to feelings that they could never have a happy marriage, so they project their unhappy biases about marriage onto others.

I admit that there *are* a lot of unhappy married people. But I think that is due to individual personalities. Some folks would be unhappy wherever they are; the marital situation may have little to do with it. A marriage, after all, can be no happier than the two individuals in it.

Building a support system of life-line friends will shorten the time it takes you to adjust to a crisis. We all need friends who can throw us a life-line when we feel we are "drowning." A friend whom we can talk with is a *real* "life-saver" during a crisis. If you have not developed such a support system, then you need to start doing so — indeed it may "save your life."

Children have a problem with friendships also, often feeling isolated and "different" — as if they are the only children of divorce in the whole school. They may not know anybody else whose parents are divorced, partly because children do not often *talk* about their parents getting divorced — it is still a stigma in many communities.

(On the other hand, there are liberal communities where the kid goes to school and says, "Guess what? My parents are getting divorced!" And the other kids say, "Welcome to the club!")

Just as their parents tend to become friends with only formerly married and single people, children may begin to seek out friendships from families with single parents. And again, children may withdraw, just as parents withdraw, and shut out all friendships whatsoever. Children who are going through the pain of their parents' divorce really need friends to talk to, but they find it difficult to seek them out or to discuss personal concerns. Schools are concerned about this, and many are providing some sort of service to help kids who shut themselves off because of their parents' divorce. It is a valuable service.

Parents can help their children find somebody to talk to. Maybe it is the time for relatives to get involved (however, relatives who are highly emotional and who may have unresolved concerns themselves are *not* good people for the children to talk to). Also, while it is often helpful for children to talk to adults, this is the time that they need to talk to other children of divorce if possible.

We need to be aware and supportive of the needs of our kids as they are going through this process. We can encourage them to become involved with others through after-school activities and community programs. Having friends to talk with will shorten children's adjustment time, just as it does for the adults involved.

Now might be a good time to sit down off the trail, rest for a moment, and take a look at the people around you. How long has it been since you have taken time to act interested in them, to see them as people rather than as married, potential lovers, or someone to be afraid of? Do any look interesting enough to have as a friend? I am sure you will find it easier to make the rest of the climb up this mountain if you have a friend to hold your hand, to give you a hug, and to catch you when you slip. Why not take time right now to invest emotionally in some friendships? If you worry about rejection, remember that that person may want a friend just as much as you do!

Use the check list below to assess your progress with friendships, before you go on to the next chapter. Remember too, that friendship does not just *happen* — like anything worthwhile, it takes continuous effort!

1. *I am relating with friends in many new ways since my crisis.*
2. *I have at least one life-line friend of the same sex.*
3. *I have at least one life-line friend of the opposite sex.*
4. *I am satisfied with my present social relationships.*
5. *I have close friends who know and understand me.*
6. *People seem to enjoy being with me.*
7. *I have both single and married friends.*
8. *I have discussed ideas from this book with an important friend.*
9. *I communicate frequently about important concerns with a close friend.*

LEFTOVERS:
They're Not All in the Refrigerator!

Earlier experiences are extremely influential in your life; and the attitudes and feelings you develop in relationships with parents, family, friends, and lovers are bound to carry over into new relationships. Some of these attitudes and feelings are helpful in new relationships, others are not. A common leftover problem, even for adults, is an unresolved need to rebel against prior constraints, such as parental rules. Recognize the valuable leftovers, so you can keep and nourish them; work at changing those which get in the way.

chapter ten

Thelma was talking about how hard it was to parent her son. "Sometimes he sounds like his father when he criticizes me, and I just can't help but fly off the handle at him. It's not fair for me to do that, but I can't seem to stop it."

Steve reported that he grew up with a father who always criticized him to his face but then would tell others how proud he was of his son. He decided that he wanted to be praised to his face so he married a woman whom he thought would give him a lot of "warm fuzzies." After a period of time in the marriage, he realized that he had married a critical woman even though he had tried not to. "I don't understand how that happened — I never thought I'd marry someone like my father."

Rick and Joan had a very respectable marriage, with a lifestyle very much like that of their parents. Suddenly Joan's behavior changed. She began to associate with a younger crowd, started all kinds of new activities which she had never tried before, and took more and more time for herself, apart from the marriage. One day she reported to Rick that she felt too confined in the marriage, and that she was going to have to go off and "get her head on straight."

We're well over halfway up the mountain now, and it is time to make a careful inspection of our packs, before we proceed to the top. Many of us may be carrying extra, unneeded weight. I am reminded of a story told me by a friend who, on his first backpacking trip, carried a quart of water to the campsite at 11,000 feet in the Sierra Nevada Mountains. When he arrived at the top, he realized that, for the last five miles, he had been carrying an extra two pounds of *water* while climbing through *snow!*

Are you lugging an unnecessary load of leftovers from earlier days? You may have learned to carry extra weight in your past marriage, or perhaps in your relationships with parents, school, friends, or others while you grew up. It is time now to unload those unneeded burdens!

You may have thought that you left all the old hangups behind in your former marriage. Maybe you did not notice that you still had them until a new love-partner came along and looked in your backpack to see what you were carrying. Well, join the large crowd: people who believed that all they had to do was become involved in

117

another love-relationship. They thought that all the old hassles
would go away with the former spouse; instead they found the same
hassles were still plaguing them.

Our relationships with others are partially an attempt to fill up the
deficiencies in ourselves. We develop a pattern of interaction, based
upon such feelings as rejection, loneliness, a need to feel guilty, or
on a more positive note, feelings of happiness. We act out our
feelings in relationships with others.

I have mentioned my earlier work as a juvenile probation officer. I
often worked with teenagers — usually girls — who had run away
from home. I learned that when the teenager left home, she believed that the problem was in the home and that if she could just
get away, the problem would be solved. It normally took from three
days to three months (there seemed to be something "magical"
about three months) for the teenager to learn that *some* of the problem was *within her*. At that point it became possible to work with the
teenager in order to help her make the changes in her pattern of
interaction with others.

Many people who are divorcing are like runaway teenagers: "The
grass will be greener on the other side of the fence." More dumpers
than dumpees seem to follow the runaway syndrome. It often takes
another relationship for the runaway divorced person to realize that
the problem is within both him/herself and the former love-partner.
When that insight is gained, it is time to begin the personal growth
needed to overcome the leftover problem.

One good example of a burdensome leftover is one I like to call the
stray cat syndrome. Carolyn is a woman who has learned to bring
home stray cats — probably has been doing it since childhood. She
feels so good when she is able to play "Florence Nightingale." Then
the stray cat starts drinking a little too much. Carolyn tries harder to
rescue him from the perils of alcohol. He drinks more (after all he is
getting a lot of attention for drinking!). Finally, when she reaches
her martyr's tolerance limit, Carolyn leaves the marriage (or maybe
he leaves); then she proclaims loudly to everyone how good it feels
not to be taking care of that drunken bum. She starts dating, finds a
guy that she is sure "will never be an alcoholic," and marries him.
The pattern starts repeating, and he begins drinking too much.
Carolyn again provides care, giving him his "milk in a saucer"

every evening when he comes home. One day it suddenly strikes her, "I married another alcoholic!"

Carolyn seems to have a need *within her* to take care of stray cats. It makes her feel good. She will continue, either consciously or unconsciously, to *need* to take care of another. It is easy to see the critical need to examine our leftover patterns and to discard those which are really hurting us and our relationships.

Often a new relationship will provide a method of working on the leftovers. A leftover may rise up and strike you; you may become angry at that person and express your irritation. He or she reacts, "Those comments don't fit me. I don't know what you're talking about. I'm listening to what you say but it just doesn't seem to apply to me. Perhaps it's *your* problem?"

If you are aware of your feelings and the voices talking inside you, you may be able to express your irritation and then tie it into an earlier relationship. Sometimes people even use the old person's name in their anger, and that is a real clue to where the problem is coming from. Listen to the voices, do some reflecting, and when the new friend says that does not fit him/her, try to discover who it does fit. When you begin to recognize who it is you are actually angry with, analyze your feelings for insight into what makes you behave this way. Communication with another person is helpful at this time because it provides a sounding board to bounce your feelings off, just as the wall on the handball court bounces the ball back — and demands that *you* handle the ball.

Fred talked at one seminar about the way his ex insisted on keeping the house so immaculate that he did not feel comfortable living there. As he expressed this anger in the class, Gloria took up the role of Fred's former wife: "But that was the only way I could please you. I didn't feel capable of making you happy in bed, or pleasing you in the way I treated our children. So I buried myself in housework, making sure that I could please you with an extra clean house." Fred was able to see that his unhappiness was connected with her keeping an immaculate house. If he could have been happy and expressed it to her, she would not have felt the pressures to perform. Gloria provided him with a chance to bounce his feelings and attitudes off another person; and he was able to see himself more clearly, as if looking in a mirror.

I want to emphasize the importance of good communication in dealing with relationship difficulties. If you are not able to understand your feelings, and not able to communicate these feelings to another, then in future relationships you will probably not be able to deal with leftovers any better than you did in the past. However, if you become aware that a stale, old leftover has arisen in your relationship, and if you acknowledge it, admit it, and talk about it, then you may be able to get rid of it by dealing with it openly. Open, honest communication is not only invaluable in current relationships, it also helps a person to identify, deal with, and remove leftovers from the past.

One of the most common leftovers we carry from our earlier experiences is the unresolved need to establish ourselves as independent persons by rebelling against our parents and their rules for us. If we carry that particular burden into adult relationships, it can seriously jeopardize any romance!

There is a period of rebellion in each teenager's growth when the not-quite-adult is seeking an individual identity. Although it is a necessary part of young adult development, it causes a tremendous strain in the family relationship. I saw many young people on probation while they were going through this *rebel stage*.

When I began working with people going through the divorce process, I put the theory of rebellion on the shelf. Nevertheless, over time, it began to dawn on me that it is not just teenagers who are rebelling, but that many times adults of all ages are going through a stage very similar to the adolescent's rebellion. When adults do go through this rebel stage, it causes a tremendous strain in the marriage relationship, and often it is the beginning of the end of the marriage.

Why are there so many people stuck in this portion of the climb? They appear very uneasy. Maybe they lack confidence in their ability to climb this steep part of the trail. Is confidence so difficult to gain? How difficult is the discovery of one's identity?

Sally, a teenager I counseled, was struggling to discover who she was, and what she wanted to become. She complained about the difficulty of the struggle and how much energy it required. I assured her that this identity struggle is especially appropriate as a teenager. Indeed, many adults have not resolved the struggle. "Why do people wait so long to find themselves?'' she asked. When I reminded her how difficult and scary the search is, she replied with teenage wisdom, ''Perhaps many people are afraid to become *themselves!*''

Sally was right. Many people continue to conform to the wishes of their parents and society, so they never gain their own identities. They marry because society expects it (another common cause of divorce). Internal pressures urge people to become themselves and stop pleasing everyone else. But after marriage they may feel confined in a shell, and begin to feel the need for freedom and an identity of their own. They start rebelling in attempts to develop an independent identity. That puts great strain upon the marriage, and often places the spouse in a parent role. They may feel they want to be free of the *marriage,* but in reality they want to be free of *parental control. They dump the spouse when in reality they are trying to dump the parent!* Because their behavior often becomes radically different, these people themselves — and those around them — wonder what has happened. If the rebellious behavior can be seen as a way to gain an identity, then it may be more easily understood and accepted.

Hopefully these people will grow emotionally, and will develop their own identities. Behavior which will please themselves, rather than attempting to please others, is likely to be much more satisfying and successful. Much of my marriage counseling centers around this problem of one partner's rebellious behavior and the resulting strains on the marriage. This rebellious time can be a period of tremendous personal growth. But the progress is often not apparent to others, who see the rebel as irresponsibly ''goofing around.''

Recently in my two classes of about 40 people, I described this theory of rebellion. About 30 of the 40 people there stated that they saw their spouse going through this rebel stage just before they left the marriage! It appears to be a very major cause of divorce (is that #19?). In trying to dump expectations put on them by parents and significant adults in their lives, rebels end up dumping the love-partner instead. The whole situation is both so common and so unfair that it warrants a detailed attempt to understand just what is going on.

I have observed three stages of growth and development, which I call the *shell stage*, the *rebel stage,* and the *love stage*. The *shell stage* occurs when we are young, conforming and trying to please our parents. During these years, children have the same moral and political values, belong to the same church, and more or less behave in ways expected of them by their parents. The shell stage child is basically a reflection of the parents, similar to the egg that is laid by a chicken, with no identity of his/her own. Vocabulary of people in the shell stage is full of inhibitions: "What will people think? I must be careful to do what I'm supposed to do. I should follow the rules and regulations of society. I must conform to what society expects from me."

In the teen years, or sometimes later, a person begins a period of rebellion, breaking out of the shell. This *rebel stage* includes changed behavior, doing what one "should not" do, pushing against the limits, and trying to find out how far one can go. It is very experimental at this stage, and the person is trying out different kinds of behavior. The little chicken inside is growing, beginning a life of its own, and starting to pick its way out of the shell. Vocabulary of the rebel stage is: "I've got to do it on my own. I don't need your help. If it weren't for you, I would be able to be the person I want to be. Please leave me alone!"

Later, as the person begins to get through the rebel stage and find an identity of his or her own, the young chicken suddenly emerges entirely separate from the parental egg. I call this stage the *love stage*.

My father has a story (also attributed to Mark Twain by some) to illustrate the process: When Dad was a freshman in high school, his father was dumb and stupid. But by the time he graduated, he could not believe how much his father had learned! Grandfather, of course, had not changed as much as Dad had during those years.

The vocabulary of the love stage are words of acceptance and understanding. "My parents did the best they could. They made mistakes and many times I was angry and upset with them, but they've tried and they've done the best they could. I understand and accept them for what they are." I call this adult period the *love stage* because the person has an independent identity, and is capable of loving another person as an adult rather than because of childish expectations.

In the shell stage, one does what one *should do;* in the rebel stage, what one *should not do;* and in the love stage, what one *wants to do.* Many times behavior in the love stage will be similar to behavior in the shell stage, but the motivation behind it is entirely different. Instead of trying to please somebody else, the person is trying to please her- or himself.

"That's all nice *theory,*" you may be saying, "but what does it have to do with *rebuilding?*" Well, as it happens, many marriages are built on a foundation of immaturity, with one partner stuck in the shell stage, spending his or her whole life trying to please and do what others want. Eventually, the shell partner gets fed up with this role. The pressures of inevitable personal growth become so great that the person's behavior changes, sometimes radically, like a volcanic eruption. This major shift by the formerly compliant partner puts a tremendous strain on the relationship. The shell stage partner has broken out of the shell, into the rebel stage, by rebelling against the love-partner.

I have prepared a chart summary of the progression through these three stages, Figure 10-1 on page 124. The chart shows some typical characteristics of the stages: *vocabulary, behavior,* and *growth steps* one may find helpful. Please recognize that these are highly individual. Although some patterns exist, each individual will be unique!

Members of my seminar groups over the years have provided many examples of the shell/rebel/love phenomenon.

Eloise came to class very angry one night because her ex, Larry, was going through the rebel stage and causing her a lot of unhappiness. Larry had been a school principal when he was in the shell stage; but because he was looking for less administrative responsibility, he returned to full-time teaching. He developed a relationship with a woman involving "a lot of communication," helping him to find out "who he was." Larry was, of course, very excited about this new relationship. After his young son came to visit, Larry sent him home with a suitcase full of clothes and a note explaining to Eloise how great his new relationship was. Needless to say, this made her extremely angry! As it happened, we were discussing the rebel stage that week in the seminar. Eloise began to understand what was happening with Larry and his attempt to grow

Figure 10-1. "BECOMING AN ADULT" IN THREE NOT-SO-EASY STAGES

	SHELL ◯	REBEL ⚡	LOVE 🐣
VOCABULARY	"What should I do?" "I'll do whatever you want." "Take care of me." "You're everything to me." "I only want you to be happy."	"If it weren't for you..." "I don't need your help!" "Leave me alone!" "I'll do it anyway." "If it feels good, do it!"	"I've considered the alternatives." "I'll take responsibility for my choice." "It may not work, but I want to try." "You and I can both enjoy ourselves."
BEHAVIOR	Compliant, obedient. Caregiving [obliged]. Consistent, predictable. Careful, non-risking. Obligations, not choices.	Self-centered, selfish. Irresponsible, blames others. Erratic, unpredictable, careless Childish, "plays" with young folk. Sports cars, flashy clothes, sex	Self-enhancing, respects others. Responsible, flexible, open. Willing to risk, learns from mistakes. Makes choices based on facts.
GROWTH STEPS self	Begin to trust self. Begin to take risks. Begin to communicate openly. Begin to accept responsibility. Begin to try new behavior.	Try positive growth activities: classes, recreation, exercise, friendships, hobbies, community. Enter therapy [with spouse?]. Talk to spouse, friend, therapist Maintain moral, ethical balance	Work at self-awareness. Work at self-acceptance. Work at open, honest communication. Develop close, non-romantic friends Express anger assertively. Maintain balance of independence and interdependence in close relationships.
partner	Encourage partner's growth. Lessen dependence on partner. Cooperate in therapy if needed Prepare for turbulence when "rebellion" starts!	Maintain stability, patience. Allow partner to grow up. Be available to talk with partner Encourage joint therapy. Recognize rebellion is against shell, not you!	

up and leave some of the old leftovers. She was able to let go of some of her anger as she gained an understanding of what was happening.

Gretchen became very excited as I explained this theory in class. Her husband had been a college professor and had proceeded to run off with one of his students while he was in the rebel stage. The whole thing seemed insane to her, until she heard the shell/rebel/love theory of growth and development. When she recognized that Charles was trying to get free from past expectations and become a person of his own identity, Gretchen was able to see that there was some sanity in what had appeared to be insanity.

Bill told the group that three years ago his marriage suffered a crisis while his wife was going through the rebel stage. When he and Charlotte went for marriage counseling, the therapist put a damper on the rebel stage and pushed Charlotte to "behave as she should" — in effect telling her to remain in the shell stage. Bill said he felt this was a mistake at the time. The marriage lasted another three years until suddenly Charlotte's growth pressures and need to rebel surfaced again, and she became "completely irresponsible," leaving the marriage and the home without even taking any clothes! Bill did not hear from Charlotte for three weeks. Looking back on those painful events, Bill observed that maybe people need to be concerned about what stage of growth and development their *therapists* are in!

Many people ask — if so many marriages end when one person is going through the rebel stage, is there any way to have the relationship *last* when a person is going through the rebel stage? The rebel who can focus inward and realize the internal interaction going on between him- or herself and the parental figures of the past can deal directly with the *shoulds,* the *oughts,* and the *expectations.* To talk about one's rebellion rather than acting it out will be much less destructive to those near and dear at the present!

I believe it is possible for a person to find the emotional space *within* a marriage to rebel, perhaps by becoming involved in therapy, college classes, community service, recreational or sports programs, or other creative activities. The rebel needs opportunities to experiment with behavior, to try new styles of relating, and to interact with people other than the spouse. If the couple can under-

stand directly what is happening — that the rebel is working on an
internal conflict which has little to do with the spouse — it can free
the work of growth and development to be done *within* the person,
rather than strain the love-relationship.

Leftovers, particularly those involving unresolved internal conflicts, can be a source of much pain in relationships. If you or your
partner is struggling with rebellion, admit it, accept responsibility
for it, and find a healthy relationship (with a therapist if necessary)
to help you get it out of your system.

Children will have some difficulty with leftovers, similar to their
parents. The child's style of interaction with others is based on only
a few years of life experience, and a limited repertoire of behaviors.
A strong influence right now is the feeling of internal pain. So until
the child changes, he or she will continue to interact with adults as
before. If a new stepparent comes into the picture, for example, the
child will tend to have the same problems with that stepparent as
he/she had with his/her natural parent. This will not change until
the child works through those old emotions, and learns new ways of
relating to adults.

The one common characteristic of leftovers is that *they are left
over* from past relationships and often have little to do with the
present relationship. We carry these feelings and attitudes from the
past within us, and we often express them in our current relationships with others. Extra baggage, unneeded weight, the leftovers
that we do not deal with will surely cause troubles in future relationships — romantic or with friends and relatives. It can be hard to
work out those internal conflicts without a special relationship
to help. A therapist, a group, a trusted friend, or even a stable love-
relationship can help one carry our the emotional garbage.

Next time you see a person on the trail acting like a teenager,
rebelling and always angry at parental, authoritative figures, you
can be understanding. You know that rebel is trying to grow up
emotionally, to gain an independent identity, and to become free
from past expectations and controls. Even though you may want to
become parental and tell the rebel how to behave, maybe you need
to back off, remain adult yourself, and say, ''I think that's probably

the best thing for where he or she is right now.'' Indeed, perhaps you are still in the shell stage yourself, needing to start some rebellion of your own to improve your sense of self-worth and to find a better identity!

Do you notice that you are really making progress in the climb up the mountain? The fact that you are able to face and deal with leftovers is an indication that you are getting a much broader perspective of life and yourself. You probably could not have done much about carrying out the leftovers when you were at the bottom of the mountain trying to survive emotionally.

After you make sure you are ready by responding to the check list below, go on to the next part of the journey. We will take a look at that elusive but ever-present phenomenon, *love*.

1. *I am aware of the leftovers I am carrying from past relationships.*
2. *I am working on my leftovers rather than blaming others for them.*
3. *I am building relationships that will help me eliminate my leftovers.*
4. *I understand that I will have to change attitudes and awareness within me in order to rid myself of leftovers.*
5. *I am avoiding becoming emotionally involved with stray cats.*
6. *I have identified whether I am in the shell, rebel, or love stage in my growth and development.*
7. *I have thought about my spouse's growth and development in terms of the shell, rebel, and love stages.*
8. *I have thought about my parents' development in terms of the shell, rebel, and love stages.*
9. *I have identified positive ways of rebelling in contrast to more negative, destructive forms of rebelling.*
10. *I can understand and accept those elements of my spouse's behavior which were related to the rebel stage.*
11. *I realize the shell, rebel, and love stages are something that may happen several times in my life.*
12. *I am attempting to do the self-care needed to remain strong and stable.*
13. *I will attempt to get rid of as many leftovers as possible before I get into another long-term, committed love-relationship.*

LOVE Thyself As Thy Neighbor

Many people need to relearn how to love, in order to love more maturely. Your capacity to love others is closely related to your capacity to love yourself. And learning to love yourself is not selfish and conceited. In fact, it is the most mentally healthy thing you can do. There are a number of specific steps you can take to increase your self-love.

chapter eleven

Love is like bouquet of roses: you don't remember the work to get them; you only remember the love in her eyes when she received them.

Love is like sitting with my back to the fireplace. I can feel the warmth without ever seeing the fire.

Love is the greatest gift you can receive. But you have to give it to yourself.

Ed

As we make our way up the mountain, we observe graffiti on the rocks, written by poets commenting about love. Most of what we learn about love *is* from the poets. Who had any homework in school concerning the nature of love? Would you take time right now to do some ''homework?'' In the space below write your definition of what love is. (I am talking about love between two people in a romantic relationship, not about parental love, spiritual love, or love for humankind.)
LOVE IS:

Okay, when you are done, turn the page and continue reading.

I have asked hundreds of people to do this exercise in the divorce adjustment seminars. It is a very difficult assignment for divorced people — or for anyone, for that matter. A typical divorced person says, "I thought I knew what love is, but I guess I don't." Many people feel inadequate about the definition of love. Love is like a diamond. You can view it from many different directions, and there is no right or wrong way of defining it. There is only the way you feel about love.

In our society many people have stereotyped love to be something you do *for* somebody or *to* somebody. Very few people have learned that love is something that should be centered *within you,* and that the basis for loving others is the love you have for yourself. Most of us recall the instruction in the Bible to "Love thy neighbor as thyself." But what if you do not love yourself?

Here is a somewhat cynical definition upon which many relationships are based: "Love is the warm feeling that you get toward somebody who meets your neurotic needs." This is a definition of *neediness* rather than love. Because we are not whole and complete people, but have emotional deficiencies, we try to fill those emotional deficiencies by "loving" another person. What we lack in ourselves we hope to find in the other person. In other words, many of us are *half people* trying to love someone in order to become whole. My belief is that love coming from a whole person is more mature.

Perhaps you have heard the expression "warm fuzzies with a fish hook in them." A *warm fuzzy* is a nice gesture that you give somebody — such as saying, "I love you." Unfortunately, many of us are still struggling to fulfill *ourselves*. If my own life bucket is empty when I say, "I love you," to another person, it probably means, "Please love me." The other person finds the warm fuzzy, swallows it, and is hooked. Saying "I love you" from an empty bucket tends to be manipulative, while love from a full bucket allows others to be themselves and to be free.

Another problem in our society is that *falling in love* is the most acceptable reason for getting married. However, *falling in love* may have more to do with loneliness than with warmth toward the other person. Falling in love to overcome loneliness is not actually love. It is rather a feeling of warmth which comes from breaking down the barriers that have kept us from being intimate with other people.

Sometimes one does not love the other person, but loves instead the *idealized image* of that person. When the difference is realized, one becomes disillusioned, falls out of love, and the relationship is dissolved. If a couple can grow past the stage of loving their idealized images of each other, there is a possibility that they will be able to love in a more mature manner. For some, this growth will occur in the love-relationship, and their love for each other will mature. For others, maturity comes only after dissolution of an immature relationship.

I see many people loving with an immature love: Love equals doing something *to* somebody or *for* somebody; Love equals taking care of someone; Love equals achieving; Love equals always being in control; Love equals "never having to say you're sorry;" Love equals always being strong; Love equals being nice.

Shirley had believed that love equals being nice, and she was trying to improve an unhealthy love-relationship. Ken asked her in class why it was not working for her to be nice. Shirley replied, "I guess I just wasn't nice *enough*."

Many (most?) of us, while growing up, have not received enough *unconditional love* — love that was given by parents or others just because we *were*, not because we *earned* it by being "good." We adopt immature forms of love toward others because we have not been loved unconditionally. That is a tough history to overcome. Nevertheless we can come to realize that mature love equals loving yourself for being what you are, and likewise loving another person for who he or she is. When we can feel such unconditional no-matter-how-you-act love, we have learned what I call mature love. Mature love allows you fully to be yourself with the loved one.

For many people it is difficult to give up the immature forms of love. That is the way they have always received their strokes, attention, and good feelings. Yet, eventually they recognize that they had to keep striving harder in order to earn the love they were seeking. It is like settling for second best, taking whatever strokes we can, rather than going all the way to get really good strokes by learning to love ourselves.

Look at the definition of love that you wrote at the beginning of this chapter. In my classes, most people include in their definition of love something that makes the love *other* centered — centered in

the other person rather than within themselves. Many people write
that love is caring and giving and making that other person happy.
Very few people include in their definition of love a mature idea of
self-love.

Let us examine that. If the center of your love is in your partner
and the relationship dissolves, the center is suddenly removed; and,
as we considered in chapter five, this makes divorce even more
painful. What might it be like if you had become a whole person and
learned to love yourself? If divorce came, there would still be pain
and trauma. But it would not be so devastating; you would still be a
whole person.

Divorce is especially traumatic for those who have not centered
their love within themselves and learned to love themselves. They
end up feeling unlovable, or that they are incapable of loving another person. Many spend a great deal of time and energy trying to
prove to themselves that they are lovable. They may search for another love-relationship immediately, because that helps to heal the
wound. They may become sexually promiscuous, developing all
kinds of relationships with anybody who comes along. Many of
these people have confused sex and love, feeling that if they go out
and find sex, with it will come the love they have been missing and
needing. I sometimes think it would be more appropriate for them to
say, "I sex you," rather than, "I love you"! As I discussed in chapter nine, it is wiser to go easy on the love-relationships during this
difficult time. Invest in friendships instead, until you have made
good progress at learning to love yourself.

The Beatles' line, "All the lonely people — where do they all
come from?," expresses well the vital needs of so many people who
have never really learned to love and to be loved. Sometimes it
seems easier to love others, and not allow oneself to be loved. By
"wanting to love another person," you may really be hiding your
own need to be loved.

That need to be loved unconditionally is not met very often. As a
child, parents' love can be seen as unconditional. After all, virtually
all parents are able to provide the basics of food, clothing, shelter,
care, and physical affection. The child's limited awareness makes
this seem to be unconditional love. The child has no question that
this love is infinite and omnipotent.

However, with age, maturity, and awareness, one recognizes that any human being may at any point stop loving another for any reason. Or the love may be ended by death. For adults it is difficult to emotionally accept *unconditional* love. Perhaps you can attack the problem from another direction: by learning to love yourself unconditionally. Sound like "pull yourself up by your bootstraps?" Actually it is simply an acceptance of yourself for what you are: a unique individual, with no one else like you. You can begin to feel that you are an *okay* person, and begin to feel love for *yourself.*

It is difficult to love yourself if you have not been loved as a child. This is where a spiritual relationship can become very important. If you can develop faith in a Supreme Being who gives the unconditional love that you have difficulty accepting within yourself, then you have experienced one of the greatest values of spiritual life. The omnipotent God loves us for what we are, not for what we do to or for somebody. The person who has developed a spiritual relationship with a Supreme Being, can in turn feel loved unconditionally. He or she will also have the potential to love others in the same way.

Psychologists place a great deal of emphasis upon the diagnosis of "personalities." One way of looking at psychological diagnoses is that *they are all trying to define different ways that people are compensating for the lack of unconditional love.* If we could peel all of the psychological diagnoses down to the heart and core, we would find that the problem is basically that people have not learned to love and be loved.

We tend to teach our children the same concept of love that we learned ourselves. Thus, if you have developed an immature form of love, your children may tend to develop an immature form of love also. If you want to teach your children to love in a mature way and to make them feel loved unconditionally, you will have to learn to love yourself! *Then* you can develop the capacity to love your children so that they feel loved unconditionally.

I am emphasizing unconditional love so strongly because it is such a very vital quality for human growth. To know that I am valuable enough — just because I am me — to be loved regardless of how I act, is the greatest gift I can give myself and my children.

I would like to share a personal experience that happened to me as I was working through the divorce process. I was taking part in a meditation exercise. We sat with our eyes closed and meditated to bring a flow of energy through the different levels of our bodies until it reached the tops of our heads. I was able to follow this meditation and feel a warm flow of energy within me, gradually rising higher in my body. When the guided fantasy had reached the level of our chests, the leader said, "Many of you at this point will be feeling that the flow of energy is leaking out the front of your chests. If you are feeling such a leak, then imagine a cover over the front of your chest so that the warm flow of energy will not leak out." She was describing exactly the way I felt! I was amazed!

After the guided fantasy was over, I asked, "How did you know how I was feeling when I was sitting there with my eyes closed, not talking?" She replied that many people have the feeling that the flow of energy is leaking out the front of their chests. She related it to be belief that love is doing something to somebody or for somebody, and that it is other-centered rather than centered within ourselves. Thus the flow of energy leaks out toward others. We emotionally drain ourselves by putting the love into others, rather than filling our own bucket of life.

I thought about this a great deal and decided that my goal was to learn to love myself in a more adequate manner. I decided that I would like to have my love be a warm glow, burning within me, warming me and the people with whom I came in contact. My friends would be warm without having to prove that they were lovable. They simply would feel warm by being close to my fire!

Since a special, committed love-relationship involves being *very* close, that special person gets an extra flow of warmth from my fire.

How about you? Do you have a fire going within you? Or has your fire gone out? I think it is important for us to care for the fire within us and make sure that we have a glow that warms us and also allows the people around us to be warm.

Let us sit and rest on the trail, and meditate for a while. Have you ever watched a cow chew her cud? I always wonder what a cow is thinking then because she looks so contented. Let us be contented like that for a while and think about an important concept. *Our lives express our definition of love.* If we believe that love is translated as *making money,* then that is how we spend our time. We act out our definition of love in our behavior. How have you been acting out your definition of love? What has been the important priority in your life? Are you satisfied with the definition of love you act out by your behavior, or do you want to change? Think about it.

An interesting paradox exists about the way we love another person. While each of us has a unique style of loving, each person tends to believe that his or her style is *the only way there is* of loving! It is difficult for us to see that there are styles other than our own. When you enter into a love-relationship it is important to be aware of your own style, and also that of the other person. Perhaps by examining some of these styles we can better understand ourselves and others.

The *romantic* style of loving has a lot of warmth, feeling, and emotion. It is the "electricity" type of love, sending all kinds of tingly feelings through your body when you see the beloved person (you actually do have physiological changes in your body, such as increases in heart beat and body temperature). This tends to be an idealistic type of love, leading you to search for and find the "one and only" person for whom you can feel it. Many of our popular songs refer to this style of love. The romantic lover tends to love deeply and to need a sexual relationship along with romantic love. Withholding sex from a romantic lover is sometimes compared to withholding food from a baby. It is an important part of this style of loving. Because it is so loaded with feeling and emotion, romantic love may not be as stable as some of the other styles of loving.

Friendship love is not as loaded with emotion and feeling. The relationship starts with a liking for each other, and then the liking "just sort of grows" into something more, which might be called love. It is cooler, lacking the passion of romantic love. Sex is not as important to the friendship lover, often developing long after the relationship has started. This is one of the most stable styles of loving, and it is not unusual for people who get into this style of loving to remain good friends even if they divorce. Their loving was based upon mutual respect and friendship rather than strong emotional feelings.

Game-playing love regards the love-relationship as a game with certain rules to follow. Game players are not as interested in intimacy as romantic lovers. In fact, they may have several simultaneous love-relationships in order to avoid closeness and intimacy.

Game-playing love is like the popular song that says, "When the one you love is gone, love the one you're with." Game-playing lovers tend to make up their own special rules, and their sexual relationships will follow whatever rules are most convenient.

There is a *needy* style of loving that tends to be full of possessiveness and dependency. This style of loving is very emotional, and the need to be loved makes it very unstable. The people involved tend to have difficulty maintaining the relationship; and they feel a lot of jealousy, possessiveness, and insecurity. Many people who have been through the divorce trauma adopt this style of loving because it reflects the neediness resulting from the divorce pain. Especially typical of the first relationship after the separation: "I've got to have another love-relationship in order to be happy." This is an immature style of dependent and possessive love.

The *practical* lover takes a realistic look at the love-partner and decides, on a rational and intellectual basis, if this love is appropriate. This type of person will make sure that there is similarity in religious beliefs, political beliefs, ways of handling money, views on raising children.... The lover may look into deficiencies in the person's family by considering socioeconomic status, characteristics, and genetic makeup. The practical lover will choose to love someone whom it "makes good sense" to love.

There are *altruistic* lovers, who may be somewhat other-centered and very willing to meet the needs of the other person. Carried to the extreme, the altruistic lover may become a martyr, trying to meet his or her own empty bucket needs. There is, however, an *authentic* altruistic lover: a person who has a full bucket and enough inner strength to be able to love another person in a very unselfish manner. Many altruistic lovers have strong religious beliefs, and find a relationship with a Supreme Being keeps their own buckets full.

Each person obviously is a mixture of these styles, and there is no one style that fits us at all times. Understanding your own mixture of styles is very important when you get into a love-relationship with another person. A couple with whom I was doing marriage counseling had a great deal of difficulty because he was a friendship lover and she was a romantic lover. She felt that his *cool* love was not love, and he felt that her romantic love was *unstable*. His style of loving was to take care of her, provide for her needs, and stay with her in the marriage; and he felt that this was proof of his love for her. Her request was for him to say, "I love you," and to express different forms of romantic thoughts that would make her feel loved and romantic. His friendship love was not a good mix with her romantic love. They had difficulty in communicating and under-standing each other's viewpoints because their basic beliefs about what love was were not compatible.

As I guide people up the trail in the divorce seminars, the question often arises, "How *do* we learn to love ourselves?" As we have seen, the answer is not easy. Here is a specific exercise that will *help* with learning to love yourself, however:

Think of a time in your life when you started to make changes. It may have been when you first had difficulties in your marriage, when you first separated from your beloved, or when you started reading this book. Make a list of the changes that you have made, the personal growth you have experienced since that time, and the things you have learned about yourself, others, and life. Consider the feeling of confidence you have gained by learning these things and getting more in control of your own life. That confidence is what gives you the good feelings. The length of your list may surprise you.

Virginia Satir has devised another method of helping people learn to gain more self-love. Make a list of five adjectives that could describe you. After you have listed these five adjectives, go through and put a plus or minus sign after each word to indicate whether you think it is a positive or negative adjective. After you have done this, look at the minus adjectives and see if you can find anything positive about that particular adjective, quality, or aspect of your person-ality.

A woman in the class listed the adjective *bitchy*. When questioned about it, she stated that her husband constantly referred to her as *bitchy*. As she began to talk about it, she realized that what he called bitchiness, she called *assertiveness* — a positive way to stick up for herself. Once she understood that difference of labels, she was able to accept that as a part of herself and to feel good about it.

After all, that is what self-love is: learning to accept ourselves for what we are. As Carl Rogers stated, when we learn to accept ourselves for what we are, then that often allows us permission to grow, change, and become something different. As long as you do not accept a part of who you are, you have trouble changing that part! Does that sound like a strange paradox? We all need to discover that "it's okay to not be okay" in certain areas. We have all had traumatic experiences that have left us wounded someplace, incidents when we did not feel loved, and experiences that have left us less than whole. But those experiences are part of life and part of living. We are not perfect; we are human beings. And when we can learn to accept some of the non-okay things about us, then we feel more okay.

How does one learn to love another person? What causes the feelings of love for that other person to begin suddenly? Perhaps it was a kind and thoughtful deed he or she did; maybe by doing something that met your needs, she or he made you feel good. What would happen if you did kind and thoughtful deeds to yourself? If you would set aside a period of time tomorrow to do something that really felt good and made you feel okay about yourself, that could be a way of learning to love yourself more fully and more completely. After all, it would be *you* that was capable of doing something kind and lovable for you!

Perhaps the most important method of learning to love yourself is to *give yourself permission* to love yourself. If you can decide that it is okay, and not selfish or self-centered to love yourself, maybe you can allow yourself to go ahead and have feelings of self-love!

While everyone is concerned about what love is, **children** may feel somewhat unlovable because one parent has left. Many suffer from the fear of losing the other parent as well. At the very time when children need a great deal of parental love, parents are undergoing their own trauma and often are incapable of giving as much love to the children as they would like. Awareness of this problem and special efforts to overcome it — especially through much honest conversation with youngsters about what is going on, and reassurance that they are much loved by both parents — are much needed at this crucial time.

A mother recently told me a delightful story, one of those little vignettes in life that seem to make everything worthwhile. Her three-year-old son came down one morning and sat on the davenport. He was sitting there thinking and meditating, and suddenly popped up with, ''What do you know? It seems like everybody loves me. Isn't that nice!'' Those are special moments in life. As parents, a major goal for us is to try to help children of divorce feel that same way, even though we are going through a period of feeling unlovable ourselves.

The growth you have achieved is something that no one has done for you, so no one can take it away from you. Your life is in *your* control, through knowledge of yourself and others. To that extent, you are not at the mercy of others anymore. Let the good feelings of your growth soak into your body, and let yourself feel the warmth of what you have achieved. Let yourself just feel love for yourself for a while. It is okay to love yourself. No — it is *more* than okay — *it is the way life is meant to be!*

Check out your own self-love before you proceed to the next chapter:

1. *I feel I am lovable.*
2. *I am not afraid of being loved.*
3. *I am not afraid of loving another.*
4. *I have an understanding of what I believe love is.*
5. *I am living a lifestyle that is congruent with my definition of love.*
6. *I feel comfortable meeting my own needs rather than feeling selfish.*
7. *I am able to accept love from others.*
8. *I am able to express love to others in a way that makes them feel loved.*
9. *I am able to love myself.*
10. *I have experienced a great deal of personal growth since my crisis began.*
11. *I am trying to develop my immature, needy, dependent parts of love into a more mature style of loving.*

TRUST:
Foundation for Healthy Relationships

If you say, "You can't trust men (women)!" you are saying more about yourself than about the opposite sex. Love-relationships after divorce often are attempts to heal your love-wound, so many of them will be transitional and short-term. In your new relationships with others, you may be reworking and improving the way you got along with your parents. By building a basic level of trust within yourself, you can experience satisfying emotionally close and intimate relationships.

chapter twelve

I was doing just fine and enjoying myself.
Then he said, "I love you."
I panicked and told him to get up,
Put on his clothes, and go home.

Ann

On this *trust* part of the trail, you will notice people who walk at a distance away from members of the opposite sex. They are like wild animals that come close, hoping to get some food, yet run for cover the minute you move toward them. These people talk about relationships a great deal of the time, and they seem to want to date and be with the opposite sex. But as soon as someone makes a move toward them, they run and shout, "Stay away!" They wear T-shirts with a motto saying, "You can't trust men (women)!" They have a severe *love-wound*.

A love-wound is the internal pain felt after the end of a love-relationship, but it may originate much earlier in life. Many of the teenagers I worked with as a juvenile probation officer suffered from a love-wound. They had learned that "love equals getting hurt." If they were put in a warm, loving foster home, they would run away. People who have a painful love-wound will emotionally distance others until the love-wound is healed. This may take months or even years for some people to heal and be able to be emotionally close again.

Relationships are important to people after divorce. When I used a questionnaire in the seminars asking participants what topics they wanted to discuss, every class picked *relationships* as the most important topic. (Have you ever noticed at a gathering of singles how often the word *relationship* is used? One woman suggested that the word be censored with a "bleep," she was so tired of hearing it! I use it a great deal in this book and in my seminars, simply because I do not know a better word with that meaning!)

141

It is often assumed that the only way to prove that you are okay is to become involved in another love-relationship. In fact, some experts in the divorce field consider remarriage an indication of *divorce adjustment.* A recent research study using the *Fisher Divorce Adjustment Scale* demonstrated the inadequacy of that assumption. A large number of remarried people have not adjusted to the past divorce.[3]

The idea that another relationship will "prove you are okay" leads many people to start immediately to find a new one-and-only. The healthiest early relationships after divorce have the goal of healing the love-wound, rather than becoming long-term, committed relationships. You have probably seen the poster that says, "You have to kiss a lot of frogs before you find a prince." It seems to be healthier to conclude, "You have to kiss a lot of frogs before you *become* a prinz." (Prinz is a non-sexist word for prince *and* princess.) If you can make this transition in your thinking, you can free these early relationships from the expectations, pressures, and futuristic thinking which makes the all important question seem to be, "Can I live with this person for the rest of my life?"

Allow your new relationships to flow in the present and to help heal your love-wound (and perhaps the other person's love-wound also). Sit back and enjoy the sunsets each day, stop to "smell the roses," let yourself heal, and realize that many of these early relationships will be short-term because they are built during a needy time in your life. Let these early relationships help you clear the confusion. You have plenty of time later to rebuild another permanent relationship when you have rebuilt a good foundation within yourself.

The divorce adjustment process may be viewed in two major steps. The first is *learning to be a single person,* ready to face life alone, with the rubble of the past cleared away. The second step is *learning to love again* after you have rebuilt your strength to carry the burden of a long-term committed relationship. If you complete step one first, step two will be easier!

Here is an exercise which will help you examine your own *style* in relationships. It is called *body sculpturing* and is derived from the work of family therapist Virginia Satir. You will need a friend to help. The diagrams illustrate different body positions which show various types of love-relationships that people have. Let's look at the body sculptures and consider the feelings underneath each of these styles:

1. A-Frame Dependency Relationship

In the dependency relationship, two people lean on each other themselves. Dependency upon another person sometimes feels good, but it is somewhat confining. When one person wants to move, change, or grow, it upsets the other who is leaning on him/her. Try this sculpture with another person and then put into words some of the feelings that you have while you are assuming this position.

2. Smothering Relationship

Here is a position quite frequently seen in teenage relationships. The vocabulary for this relationship is, "I can't live without you. I want to spend the rest of my life with you. I will devote myself completely to making you happy. It feels so good to be close to you." Many lovers start out by smothering, then gradually release the strangle hold on each other to allow more room for growth. This smothering pattern may be particularly significant during the honeymoon stage of a new love. The smothering relationship feels good for a while, but eventually the partners begin to feel trapped.

3. Pedestal Relationship

This "worshipful" relationship says, "I love you not for who you are, but for who I think you are. I have an idealized image of you and I'd like to have you live up to that image." It is very precarious on top of the pedestal because there are so many expectations to live up to. You can see the problems of communication here. In love with the person's idealized image, the worshipper is looking up to and trying to communicate with that image instead of with the real person. There is a great deal of emotional distancing inherent in this relationship, and it is difficult for the two people to become close.

4. Master/Slave Relationship

The *master* acts and is treated according to these ideas: "I'm the head of this family. I'm the boss. I'll make the decisions around here." Do not assume that this relationship necessarily places the male as the boss and head of the family. There are many females who are *masters*, making all of the decisions for their families.

In most relationships one of the partners has a personality which is at least a little stronger than the other, and that is not necessarily bad. When the relationship becomes rigid and inflexible, and one person is set up to make virtually *all* of the decisions, emotional distancing and inequality take place. Maintaining one person as master and the other as slave tends to take a great deal of emotional energy, and often results in a power struggle that interferes with the communication and intimacy of the relationship.

5. Boarding House: Back-to-Back Relationship

Linked by their elbows, these two have some sort of contract or agreement that they are going to live together. There is no communication in this relationship. The typical thing is for people to come home and sit down and watch TV while they are eating, then retire to their own living habits for the remainder of the evening. There is no expression of love toward each other. Notice as you try this position, that when one person moves forward, changes (i.e., grows and matures), the other person is linked to that change. Back-to-back is a very confining relationship. Many persons recognize this as the pattern that existed just before their relationship ended.

6. Martyr Relationship

Here is the person who completely sacrifices by trying to serve others. Always doing things for other people, never taking time for self, the martyr goes about "on hands and knees." But do not let the lowly posture fool you! The martyr position is very controlling. Note that when the person on hands and knees moves, the other person who has a foot on the martyr is thrown off balance. How does the martyr gain control? You guessed it — through guilt. How can you be angry at the person who is doing everything for you, who is taking care of you completely? The martyr is very efficient at controlling people. It is very difficult to live with a martyr because you feel too guilty to express your own needs and angry feelings. Perhaps you have a martyr parent, and can recognize ways of dealing with that parent by understanding the martyr relationship.

7. Healthy Love-Relationship

Two people who are whole and complete have happiness within themselves. Standing upright, not leaning on or tangled up with the other person, they are able to live their own lives. They have an abundance of life to share with the other person. They choose to stay together because they are free to be individuals who are sharing their lives together. They can come close together and choose the smothering position temporarily; they can walk hand-in-hand as they might do in parenting their children; they can move apart and have their own careers, their own lives, and their own friends. Their choice to stay together is out of love for each other rather than *needing* to stay together because of some unmet emotional needs. The healthy love-relationship gives both people the space to grow and become themselves.

Again, let me urge you to try these different positions with a friend and see how they feel. Speak or write about the feelings that you were experiencing while in each body position. Which of these positions describes your past love-relationship? Many people in the classes state that they think that their love-relationship went through almost all of the unhealthy body positions!

Did you learn more causes of divorce from the body sculpturing? The unhealthy relationships seem to suggest a half person looking for another half person. As you become more of a whole person (do we ever become *completely* whole?), your chances of developing a healthy, healing relationship are greatly increased.

We tend to act out our internal feelings in our relationships. If you are angry, you probably express anger in your relationships. If you are lonely, you tend to be possessive in the relationship in order to keep the other person from leaving you and making you lonely again. If you are in deep emotional pain, you will likely have a relationship full of pain. If you have a love-wound, you will emotionally distance others to avoid bumping your love-wound.

Many of us seek relationships with persons who have qualities we are missing in ourselves. If you are introverted and want to be more comfortable around people, you may marry an extrovert. Lacking confidence, you marry a person who exudes confidence. To meet your need to feel guilty, you develop a relationship with someone who will make you feel guilty.

And of course, the coin also has a positive side. If you are happy, confident, and feel lovable, you marry to act out those feelings in your relationship. We can learn much about ourselves by looking at our relationships. What feelings are you expressing in your relationships? Is there a pattern? (Do you always bring home a *stray cat?*) Do your relationships reflect good feelings within, or do they reflect neediness?

Another major factor in our relationship styles is one I've mentioned before: the interaction we had with our parents. Each of us learned how to respond to love, anger, rejection, and intimacy from our own parents. If your parents fought, then you are likely to have a very tough time with fights. If your parents were cold and untouching, then you may find it difficult to touch and handle warm

emotions. Many a marriage is not satisfactory because the partners
are interacting like their parents did.

Jeff told me, "Marriage may be like a pot of stew. If you don't
make it right the first time, you keep doing it over until you get it
right. In my first marriage, I was acting out the unproductive
patterns I learned as a child. I didn't change internally after my
divorce, so I continued to act out those patterns in my second
marriage!" If you can use each relationship to learn about yourself
and how you are acting out your internal feelings in your
relationships, you can then use each relationship to become more
the person you want to be. I think it is possible to grow from each
relationship, and that is a positive way of looking at more than one
marriage.

After divorce, we often regress and interact the way we did earlier
in life. This can be positive: becoming a healthy person emotionally
is like climbing a slide in the playground. You progress up so far,
then lose your grip and slide back down. Then the next time you are
able to climb to a higher point. Although each relationship that ends
may put you back down the slide, when you climb again, you know
how to climb higher and become more healthy. In their relationships
after divorce, many people are reworking the patterns of interaction
they learned from their parents in order to make those patterns
more productive.

I hope the body sculpturing and this discussion of various concepts of relationships are helping you carry out the rubble and make
room to rebuild yourself. The problem of trust is largely internal
rather than external, and understanding your past is helpful in
understanding where you are now. The first step of growth is to
become *aware* of ourselves, our patterns of interaction, and our
methods of relating with others. Enough of carrying out the rubble
— let us start rebuilding!

"Where do I meet someone?" is one of the questions formerly
married people ask most frequently. The simple, almost absurd,
answer is "Right where you are!" People go to bars, singles
groups, and ceramics classes (amazing how many
formerly-marrieds do that!) in their attempts to meet people. I do
not quarrel with going places where single people gather. But take
care! The "bar scene," for example, typically includes many lonely

people who cannot relate until they are slightly under the influence. And the bar hoppers are often game-players out to practice and improve their games of interaction, frequently with sex being the goal of the game. Singles groups, too, may have a certain amount of desperation and loneliness, and usually consist predominantly of women.

The question, "Where do I meet someone?" often indicates that the asker is looking for a committed, long-term partner. Perhaps somewhat desperate and sending out desperate vibrations with body language, vocabulary, and "the look in their eyes," these persons tend to drive people away. Others fear that they will become sucked in by the neediness; some call the needy ones *vacuum cleaners!*

How often have you heard it said, "There ain't nothing but turkeys out there?" Of course, it is partly true. Many formerly-married people are hurting, and are not especially attractive dates during the rough periods. But have you thought about what you would do if an *eagle* landed near you? You would probably run like mad! A person who is eligible and looks like a possible marriage partner scares the hell out of you if your love-wound is still very painful. Maybe you are *looking* for turkeys because they are safe? Maybe you are still hurting, and more or less a turkey yourself? Turkeys do tend to hang together, you know. Maybe when there "ain't nothing but turkeys out there," *you* are still a turkey and have not rebuilt yourself to the status of an eagle.

When you have blinders on and see only potential marriage partners, do you realize how many people you are not seeing out there? When you start becoming interested in getting to know the people *around you,* then you start making friends. And some of those friends *might* become lovers, but *looking* for lovers keeps both friends and lovers away! It bears repeating: Your goal (*for now*) is to get acquainted and develop friendships with the people around you. Pay no attention to whether or not they are eligible singles; notice only if they are interesting people you would like to get to know. Develop as many positive relationships with people of both sexes as you can, and if some become lovers — then it is frosting on the cake!

You can get to know these potential friends wherever you are. When you go to the grocery store and send out positive vibrations and act interested in others, you attract people like flies to honey. At parties, if you are not trying to find a bed partner or someone to go home with after the party, you might get to know a number of interesting people. If you have found happiness within and send out those vibrations, people will enjoy being with you.

I am fully aware of the difference in the numbers of formerly-married males and females. The ratio is unfair because there are so many more females than males. Women live longer than men and so for each year of life there are more females than males living. Also, there are many males who remarry someone much younger, often a woman not married before. (It may be small compensation to women, but it is true that women adjust to living alone much better than men.)

Ginger posed another issue frequently discussed in my seminars, "Everytime I go to a singles gathering, it becomes a game of 'my-place-or-yours?'" There are many singles who have not learned to deal with the opposite sex other than sexually, but that does not mean you have to narrow yourself the same way. Keep developing your personality and broadening yourself. The more interests you develop, the more interesting people you will find.

Some ideas have grown out of the divorce seminars which may help you overcome problems of trust. Many people, for example, have difficulty with *masks*. We often project an image or attitude different from what we are feeling inside. Wearing masks is one way of distancing others so they will not know the pain we are feeling. But it gets lonely behind masks. You may be afraid to take off your mask because you might get rejected, because people would find out how afraid you are underneath. I urge you to risk taking off the mask. Only when you become real, will you have the possibility of experiencing closeness and intimacy. Find a special friend, explain that you have been hiding behind a mask of being strong and in control, while underneath you have been screaming, "Won't someone listen to me? I want to tell you how much I am hurting." Instead of rejection, you will likely find a friend who really does understand. And how will you ever know unless you take the risk?

Try being really honest the next time you go out. If you are

hurting, and have a painful love-wound, explain to the person that
you want to be with him/her, but you fear you will be a wet blanket.
Do not try to put on the mask of cool and sophisticated, when in
reality you are scared to death. When you explain your fears to
others, you might be surprised to learn they were feeling the same
way! After all, we are *all* human. And you both are relieved to be
able to be yourselves instead of the ''cool cat'' you thought you had
to be.

Have you thought about learning to trust with friends rather than
lovers? If you find someone of the opposite sex with whom you can
be a *friend*, that person is much safer than a lover. When you add
romance to the ingredients of a friendship, it adds instability to the
relationship, and makes it harder to take risks and learn to trust.

We project our lack of trust upon others. I have often counseled
parents who said their teenager was not to be trusted. Valerie's
parents, for example, feared their daughter would become pregnant and would not allow her to date, even though she was a junior
in high school. I discovered that the mother had become pregnant as
a teenager, and was projecting her lack of trust in *herself* upon Valerie.

A similar event often occurs in marriage counseling. Tess told me
that her husband Andre kept checking on her to make sure she was
not having an affair. Then she discovered that Andre was having the
affair and projecting his lack of trust upon her! Like so many other
feelings, lack of trust may become a self-fulfilling prophecy. Valerie
told me she felt like she *should* become pregnant because that was
what her parents seemed to believe was going to happen. And Tess
felt she might as well have an affair if that was what Andre
suspected anyway!

The problem of *trust* is especially difficult for those **children** who
did not know what was going on with their parents' divorce, so the
children are now adjusting to a parent's absence with little or no
direct communication with that parent. If the father, for example,
suddenly leaves the family, and does not communicate why he is
leaving or the problems that the parents are having, the child may
feel deserted, and have trouble trusting that absent, noncustodial
parent. Kids really are tougher than you think, and can handle an
awful lot of direct communication and reality if parents will just take

the time to communicate with them. Parents who hide their heads and feel that they cannot share the reality of their situation with their children often create a great deal of mistrust in the children, and lose a potentially valuable source of love and support for themselves! It is a very unusual — or *very* young — child who does not know that the parents are going to get a divorce before the parents tell him/her. The more you can communicate and level with your children, the more they will trust what you have to say.

A severe love-wound leads to fear of trusting. As appealing as the warmth may be, to become close is to risk being burned again. Relationships after divorce are controlled by this lack of trust. The purpose of these relationships ought to be to learn trust again and to heal the love-wound. Thus many of the relationships are short-term. Trying to make them into something long-term often does nothing but increase the love-wound and prolong the adjustment process.

We have all learned how to interact from our love-relationships and from our parents. As adults, we may choose to improve the styles of interaction that we learned. Becoming aware of one's style is an important first step. It may also take several friendships and love-relationships to help one develop healthier styles.

We have to take risks to learn to trust. Risks may backfire and lead to rejection or misunderstanding, but risks are necessary if one is to become close and experience intimacy again. The rewards are worth the risk.

Here are some items to see how you are doing and if you are ready to continue the climb. We are nearing the top, so take care not to rush here — this rebuilding block must be securely in place before you proceed.

1. *I can trust members of the opposite sex.*
2. *I have begun to understand that men and women are much more alike than different in their responses to feelings such as love, hate, intimacy, and fear.*
3. *I can trust myself and my feelings.*
4. *I trust my feelings enough to act on them.*
5. *I am not afraid of becoming emotionally close to a potential love-partner.*
6. *I am aware of the ways that I distance people.*

7. *I am building relationships that will help me to heal my love-wound.*
8. *I am building healing and trusting relationships with friends of both sexes.*
9. *I communicate with others where I am emotionally rather than giving mixed messages.*
10. *I understand that not everyone is capable of being trusted.*
11. *I am capable of trusting someone when it is appropriate.*
12. *I want to heal my love-wound and experience intimacy.*
13. *I am trying to live in the present in my relationships.*
14. *I realize that many of the early relationships after divorce may be short-term.*
15. *I am taking risks in my relationships by exposing my true feelings and thoughts.*
16. *I am truly interested in the friends around me rather than desperately looking for another love-relationship.*

SEXUALITY: It's Beautiful!

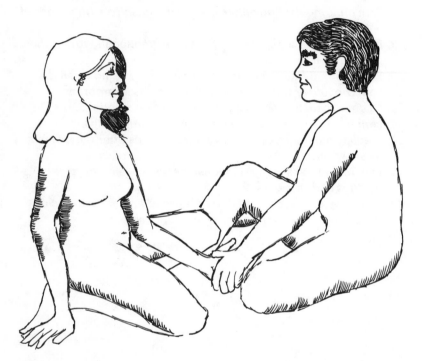

When you are first separated, it is normal to be extremely fearful of sex. However, during the adjustment process, you can develop your personal morality to express your unique sexuality. The singles subculture emphasizes authenticity, responsibility, and individuality more than rules. So you can discover what you believe rather than what is expected of you. The great difference in attitudes and values of male and female sexuality appears to be a myth. But, your adjustment could be complicated by the major changes currently taking place in female and male sex roles.

chapter thirteen

Being Divorced and Middle-aged Is:

Not taking out the garbage for fear you'll miss that obscene phone call.

Standing out in the middle of the dark parking lot and shouting, "Hey you muggers, the muggee is here."

Telling the guy who frisked you and demanded all your money that you have no money but if he'll frisk you again, you'll write him a check.

Putting a sign on your gate that reads, "All trespassers will be violated."

Looking under the bed and hoping someone is there.

Lois

Everyone looks forward to this portion of the climb with great expectations. You may have turned to read this chapter first. (If so, I urge you to read at least chapter one first!) Maybe you have been anticipating sexuality since the original discussion of the rebuilding blocks in chapter one. What was your attitude toward those *swinging singles* when you were married? Did you wonder if they were the sexual athletes they were rumored to be? And did you fantasize what it would be like to have a date with a different and exciting person each night of the week?

Now you are single. Look at the people around you. Many are spending evenings alone. Many are out pretending to have fun at a singles party — when in reality they are bored stiff. Many times you spend an evening with a person that makes your ex look attractive and desirable — and you never thought *anyone* could be worse than your ex. And everyone is going with someone and then breaking up — you can't even keep track of who is dating whom. The contrast between your fantasy of the wild single life and what it actually is adds greatly to the trauma of divorce.

Take heart — the first part of this sexuality climb is the steepest and most difficult — it gets easier after you become accustomed to being single. You have not been "out on a date" for years, and the first person you ask turns you down. You attend a singles party petrified that no one will ask you to dance — and equally petrified that someone will. At the first contact with the opposite sex you feel like an awkward junior-high kid on a first date. And wow! If someone should make a pass at you — the thought is enough to make you stay home, alone, forever.

Just what is *appropriate* behavior for an adult who has not dated in years? There were rules and chaperons at your teenage parties. You had parents to tell you what time to be in. Now you have no one to set the limits for you, and your feelings are so confused and uncertain that you cannot even rely on them. You envied the freedom of singleness, and now you would give anything to have the security of marriage again.

Later on in the process, when you have found your individual pathway, things will be more comfortable. After you have overcome your confusion and uncertainty, you will find that you can express yourself through dating and relationships with the opposite sex. There may be a freedom that you did not have when you were a teenager doing what was expected of you — or what was not expected.

In the seminars, sexuality is the last of the 10 sessions. This is not to save the best for last, but to give people time to become comfortable discussing such a personal and emotional issue. To help people become more comfortable, I ask them to write questions about sexuality — you know, the ones that they always wanted to ask but were afraid to. The questions are directed to either males or females, and the facilitator reads the questions aloud to ensure anonymity. These questions give us insights into the concerns of formerly married people.

Some questions recently separated people frequently ask include: 1) What do you find attractive and desirable in the opposite sex? 2) What do you call *going out?* I hate the word *date;* and 3) How do I tell the person I'm going out with that I don't want anything heavy?

Later on in the process, people might ask these questions: 1) What do men think about a woman who has sex early in the relationship? 2) How do women feel about having more than one sexual relationship at the same time? 3) Why don't men call again after we've gone to bed together? and 4) I refuse to consider having sex outside of marriage — would you want to go out with me?

The adjustments resulting from the changing sex roles cause difficulty for both men and women: 1) What do men think about a woman who asks you out? 2) Just what do women want? I hold the door open for one woman and she gets irritated. The next woman waits for me to open the door. What am I supposed to do? 3) I always felt comfortable making complimentary comments to a woman and asking her out. This week a liberated woman told me she liked my legs, and asked me if I would like to go out with her. What do I do? 4) Who do you think should pay for the date? and 5) Whose responsibility is it for birth control?

Questions about kids can be especially difficult: 1) Who pays for the babysitter? 2) Who takes the babysitter home? 3) What do you think about a member of the opposite sex spending the night when children are present? 4) My children don't want me to date. What do I do? 5) What do I say to my teenager when she tells me to get home early? and 6) What do I do when the kid answers the doorbell, sees me, and shuts the door in my face?

Most formerly married people are frightened about VD: 1) I would like to have sex but I'm deathly afraid of VD. How can I be sure to avoid getting VD? 2) How do I find out if the person may be infected before we have sex? and 3) What is herpes? (A majority of seminar participants are not aware of the current herpes VD epidemic.)

These questions reflect many of the concerns formerly married people have about sexuality. Dorothy reflected the emotional impact of sexuality, reporting, "I became extremely depressed last week when I realized I was 40 years old, divorced, and might never get laid again!"

I have had a conflict about having sexual relations while I am single. One part of me says that sex is important to my personal growth, and the other part says that I feel guilty having sex with a woman I'm not married to. What do I do?

Tom

On this part of the climb up the mountain you will want to find your own pathway. Each of us has an individual morality that will largely determine our direction. Because this area requires an effort not only to climb, but also to find your individual pathway, you may feel more hesitant and less confident. Take your time and make sure the pathway you choose really suits *you*. Of course, you can change paths if one is not appropriate. But some people have paid a tremendous price emotionally because they experimented with behavior that was not really compatible with their own values.

There are three stages in this rebuilding block. Each of these three stages of sexuality affects us personally a great deal as we go through the adjustment process.

You had an available sexual relationship for all those years that you were married. Suddenly, your love-relationship is not available. You are faced with all of the emotional and social adjustments of ending a love-relationship, including what to do with your sexual desires.

The first step of the process, while you are in deep grief, is a *lack of interest in sex,* or maybe a complete inability to perform sexually. Women tend to be completely uninterested in sex, men often are impotent. Just when you are feeling a great deal of emotional pain, the fact that you are uninterested or unable to perform sexually adds to the pain. Many people come to me saying, ''I was already hurting so much, and now I find that I can't perform sexually. It feels like hitting rock bottom.'' When they learn that it is perfectly normal and natural to be uninterested in sex while in deep grief, they feel greatly relieved.

Somewhere along the divorce process, perhaps near the end of the Anger rebuilding block, you get through this stage of not being able to perform sexually. At that point, you will probably go to the other extreme and reach *the horny stage.* Your sexual desires are greater than you have *ever* known in your whole life. It is almost frightening because you feel unable to control the sexual desires. Bonnie described this stage as ''delicious torture.'' Because the needs and desires of this stage are so overwhelming, it is important to understand the feelings and attitudes as much as possible.

Among the many feelings present in the horny stage is a need to prove that you are okay, personally and sexually. It is as though you are trying to solve not only your sexual problems but all of the other rebuilding blocks as well, using sex as the method. Your behavior at the horny stage may be somewhat compulsive because of this. You are trying to overcome loneliness, to feel lovable again, to improve your self-concept, to work through some anger, to develop friendships — and all of these things are concentrated in the sexual drive. It is as though your body is trying to heal itself through sexual expression alone.

I became so horny after my separation that I called my friend asking for suggestions of what I could do. Having sex with someone I was not married to was out of the question for me.

Raquel

One night stands are a popular way that people try to solve this horny stage. We see this portrayed in books and movies about divorce. The need to go out and "prove that you are okay" may be so great that you will do something sexually that you had not ever done before.

Another important understanding about the horny stage is that there is a great need for touching during this stage. As you go through the divorce process, you will probably experience a heightened need to be physically touched. Touch has remarkable, healing qualities. Depending upon the warmth and closeness of your relationship, you likely received much physical touching in your marriage. Suddenly that touching is not there anymore. Many people will try to meet their need for physical touching with sex, not realizing that there is a very real difference between physical touching and sexual touching. Although the two are entirely different, you can resolve much of your need for sexual contact by getting the physical touching that you need.

You can resolve the needs of the horny stage by methods other than direct sexual contact. If you understand that a part of the compulsive drive behind the horny stage is to prove that you are okay, and to feel good about yourself again, then you can work directly on that. Building your identity and self-confidence, and understanding

that you are lovable can overcome the loneliness and take away
some of the pressures of the horny stage. And if you can reach your
quota of hugs, this will also take away some of the pressures.
Together, these steps may go a long way toward resolving your
needs at this difficult time.

The stereotype about the divorced person being sexually an ''easy
mark'' results from the horny stage. During this period, the
divorced person *is* an easy mark. The sexual drive is tremendous.
Many people going through the divorce process have sexual relationships somewhat promiscuously.

Eventually you will overcome the horny stage and get into the
third stage of post-divorce sexuality in which your *normal sex drive*
resumes. (There is, of course, a great deal of variation in sex drive
from one person to another.) Because the horny stage is so compulsive and so controlling, people often find it a relief to be back to their
normal sexual desires.

Not everybody going through the divorce process goes through
these three stages of sexuality. Some people do not go into the celi-
bate stage of being uninterested in sex, and some do not experience
the horny stage. However, the stages are very common occurrences
which need to be recognized.

During the early stages of sexuality you are doing what you
should do; then you go through a stage of doing what you *want* to
do. Most people going through the divorce process experience the
evolution of becoming free sexually in the sense that they are
suddenly aware of who they are and what their sexual nature is.
This is another beautiful part of the divorce process.

Many people were sexually monogamous in marriage because
that is what they believed they *should* be. Then when they go
through the horny stage, they may have many sexual relationships.

*Sex in our marriage was not good. We separated and experienced sexual
relationships with other people. Then when we came together again, we
were surprised that sex with each other was good. It seemed to free us to be
apart and to be with others.*

Mike and Jane

Finally, they decide to be monogamous again because this is what they *want* to be. Consider the impact of this process upon future love-relationships. The need for sexual experience outside of a committed relationship is greatly diminished when one arrives at this third stage. As long as you are in the *should* stage sexually, there is always the temptation to do what you *should not* do. But when you reach this third stage, doing what you want to do and expressing who you really are, the temptation for sex outside a love-relationship is greatly diminished.

We have blown sex out of proportion in our society, perhaps because we hid it and denied it for so long. With so much emphasis on sex now, it appears to have lost some of its reality. Advertising is full of sex in order to sell products. We revere youth and the supposed beauty, aliveness, and sexuality of youth. With such a daily overdose in the media, it is tough to keep a proper perspective on sexuality when it comes to love-relationships and marriage.

Usually missing from popular presentations is the spiritual dimension of human sexuality. Sex is one way of transcending our normal means of expressing ourselves, and it allows us to show our love and concern for another person in a very special and positive way. Sex can be a method of transporting oneself to levels beyond *everyday*, to become something greater than what one normally is. But this spiritual dimension that is present in sexuality is also present in overcoming anger, in our ability to communicate, in learning to like another person, and in learning to accept and deal with all of the human emotions. Sexuality, when placed in perspective, may be seen as only one of the many beautiful things that occur in our expression of concern for other people.

Our society has traditionally placed extreme emphasis on having a sexual relationship only with the person to whom we are married. The messages are mixed and quite confusing. Many divorced people are amazed to learn that they can have very enjoyable and beautiful sex without being *in love* with the person. Others feel a great amount of guilt if they have sexual relationships outside of marriage. A number adopt a morality that is concerned only with not catching a social disease and not becoming pregnant.

Healthy divorce adjustment requires that we grow beyond an undue emphasis on sex and arrive at the point where we can under-

stand the beauty of our sexuality as a special way of sharing and
communicating with another person. A personal morality which
includes sexuality as an expression of your individuality and your
uniqueness, and which is concerned with the needs and well-being
of your sexual partner(s), is socially responsible, self-actualized,
and human.

To be specific, each person has to develop a personal and individual sexual morality appropriate for her or his own personality,
background, attitudes, experiences, and values. Many people will
choose to have no sexual relationships outside of marriage, and this
may be appropriate for them. Others may find sexual experiences
an appropriate way of resolving the horny stage and a way of
healing themselves after ending the love-relationship.

*I have agreed with everything you have said until now, but when you
state that experiencing sexual relationships while single can be a personal
growth experience, I have to strongly disagree. Sex is sacred, and should
occur only between two people in a sacred marriage.*

Father John

I have found that most divorced people are more comfortable
having only one sexual relationship at a time, and this can be a very
positive decision for a person to make. The evidence seems pretty
clear that most divorced people must have an emotional relationship
to support a sexual relationship. When people have communication,
trust, understanding, and respect for each other, they are comfortable having a sexual relationship. If you are able to reach this level
of self-actualization in your sexual relationships, I believe you will
find less need to have relationships outside of marriage if you
remarry in the future.

Let us now look at some of the other adjustment problems that
you may experience as you end a love-relationship and enter the
formerly married subculture. I frequently hear complaints, especially from women, that all the opposite sex is interested in is going
to bed with them. When I go to social gatherings, that is the topic of
most discussions. Yet very few formerly married people are

genuinely able to enjoy cheap and casual sex that has a lot of elements of *using*. There are, unfortunately, many people in our society who have not developed ways of interacting with the opposite sex beyond the sexual area. It can be and often is the easiest avenue open for contact and, after all, is one where the potential payoff is great. Nevertheless, there are many aspects of interaction other than sexual, and your life will be so much richer if you fully develop your range of choices. For example, in the previous chapter we looked at developing friendships with the opposite sex that are non-romantic and non-sexual.

It is interesting that, on the questionnaires in my classes asking people what they would like to talk about, the number two choice (after *relationships*) differs between men and women. The second choice for women is *sexuality* in almost all classes, and the second choice for men is *love* in almost all classes. Not only does this break up the stereotype, but in class it is very common for women to be much more comfortable talking about sexuality than men are. After one *sexuality* class, Burt confided to me that he went home and was unable to go to sleep because he was so shocked by how freely the women in the class talked about sexuality.

I believe that openness is a very healthy response style. Sexuality used to be such a sacred cow that it was impossible for people to talk and communicate about it. We were thus prevented from understanding and dealing with our sexuality. Now because of the openness, we are able to understand and develop our sexual feelings just as we understand and develop all of the other human emotions we feel.

The openness in sexual matters allows us another avenue that is very freeing. When you are dating in the formerly married society, you can discuss sexual concerns openly and early in the relationship, minimizing all of the little games that go on concerning, ''Are we going to bed or not?'' Many of the dating relationships that you have will never include sexual intimacy; it will simply not be appropriate. By discussing this and getting it out in the open, it frees you to allow the relationship to develop more naturally and normally, free of the games that go along with not knowing where you stand sexually with the other person.

If you are early in the rebuilding process, and the idea of having sexual relationships is extremely frightening, you can share this with the other person. You can say, "I really need to get out and be with a friend, but anything beyond friendship is more than I can stand emotionally at this point." You will be surprised at the favorable response from others after you have shared yourself openly like this. Most will understand and accept you because they have been through the divorce process and have experienced some of the same feelings.

Another big problem for many people entering the formerly married subculture is the question of *rules*. You may feel as though you are a bewildered teenager, not exactly understanding and knowing how to behave. There has been a great deal of change in our society regarding sexual behavior and attitudes. Most of this change is a freeing from set rules of conduct prescribed by the courting game into a freedom to be ourselves. Freedom to be yourself is very difficult if you do not know who "yourself" is. Thus the problem is not really so much that the *rules* have changed, as it is that certain behavior was *expected* before. Now you need to find your way, and follow your own unique style as you go. To become open and honest with who you are, and to express that unique individuality as much as possible, will be much more difficult than just following the established rules of dating that were prevalent before.

Another problem results from the fact that sex roles are changing, and women are initiators in everything much more than before. Women quite frequently now are expected to initiate sexual behavior, and this is all very upsetting for many people of both sexes. Women in class during the sexuality discussion ask, "How do men feel about women being the initiators?" The typical male response is that they find it very freeing to have the woman be the initiator. They have had to deal with all the fears of rejection that have been inherent in asking and initiating with women. They say that it feels good to have women now deal with the risk of being turned down, and that they are free from the burden of being the initiator all the time.

While men in the seminars talk about "how good it feels" to have women take the lead, women report that in the real world outside of the seminars, many men are threatened by assertive women. Although men say they like to be asked out, often they are uncomfortable when the actual situation arises. It appears that *intellectually* men like women to initiate, but *emotionally* men have more difficulty handling sexually assertive women.

The problem is not limited to males. Females report confusion also. The woman may say she would like to ask the man out, but when the time comes the old morality takes over and the woman never gets around to asking. For many women there is a double adjustment process happening — adjustment to becoming single, and adjustment in finding identity as a woman. It is not easy to question the old roles and try out new behavior when you are rebuilding after the loss of a relationship. On the other hand, it is an appropriate time to do it. Everything else in your life is changing. Why not try out some changes in sex roles at the same time?

Many of the new roles affect the interaction between sexes profoundly. Many women report they like the freedom of paying their own way on a date, since this frees them from the expectation of performing sexually in return for dinner. Some women enjoy responding to sexism by telling the male he has ''a nice ass.'' Some even go so far as to let men know how it feels to be used sexually, by taking them to bed, then getting up, putting on their clothes, and leaving.

It appears that the end result of the changing sex roles will be more equality between the sexes and more freedom for individuals to be themselves. Nevertheless, the period of change causes much uncertainty and confusion.

The many desperate, lonely people introduce another problem to the formerly married subculture. They make the whole problem of sexuality even more difficult because these people are basically looking for somebody to use. If you are a kind and caring person, seeing all of the *needy* people around you may tempt you to help them meet their needs, some of which may be sexual.

The great deal of loneliness and neediness out in the formerly married subculture causes special adjustment problems for those of us who are caught in the *compassion trap* — the need to nurture and give to others in response to their apparent needs. If you tend to be that way, you will have to be somewhat selfish and learn that there is no way you can meet the needs of all those who are desperate and lonely. You must meet your own needs and take care of yourself first, and do so without using other people or allowing others to use you. Do everything you can to feel good about yourself and to grow within yourself so you can become as complete and whole as possible, and can overcome your own loneliness and neediness. That will provide you a solid foundation for future relationships, and for helping others who are in *genuine* need.

Is the area of sexuality really so very different now, when you are re-entering the ranks of single persons, than it was when you were single before marriage? It *is* more open, and allows for more individual and unique expression of ourselves, rather than simply following the rules of the courting system. What you must learn in order to function in the formerly married subculture is to find yourself, express yourself, communicate, and relate with others without losing your identity. In short, simply learn to be yourself in your interactions with others, including your sexual contacts. Sexuality — as it always has been — is an important part of learning to be and to express yourself.

Children of divorce also have the rebuilding block of sexuality to deal with. When their parents' relationship ends, where do children find role models for relationships, sexuality, becoming an adult man or woman and a mature person?

It is often confusing for children to see their parents get involved in another love-relationship. Somehow children sense that it may include sex. (I think kids know more about which parents are going to bed and which are not than the parents believe!) And if the parents are in the *horny stage* and sending out all of the sexual vibrations which accompany that stage, what do the children do with that? How do they handle this new behavior in their parents?

Communication may sound like an old answer, but it is critically important at this point. When parents talk with their children *frankly* and *openly* about sexuality, it is very helpful for the kids and for the parents. Although there is much anxiety and insecurity in the children's lives, that very turmoil can be the beginning of learning. Children may well gain a far deeper understanding of sexuality — including their own — as their parents go through this stage of rebuilding.

Children can find role models in relatives, grandparents, and their parents' male and female friends. As one teenager stated to me, "It seems I've got more models around now than I ever had before!"

We have covered a lot of ground in this chapter, and there is much we have not explored. Sex is often a stumbling block for the divorced person, so be sure you have dealt thoroughly with these issues before you go on. Here are some trail markers for assessing your progress.

1. *I am comfortable going out with potential love-partners.*
2. *I know and can explain my present moral attitudes and values.*
3. *I feel capable of having a deep and meaningful sexual relationship if it were appropriate.*
4. *I would feel comfortable being intimate with another love-partner.*
5. *My sexual behavior is consistent with my morality.*
6. *I am satisfied with my present dating situation.*
7. *I am behaving morally the way I would like to have my children behave.*
8. *I believe that my personal sexuality expresses my individual and unique morality.*
9. *I feel satisfied with the way I am meeting my sexual needs.*
10. *I take responsibility for my interaction with others.*
11. *I have learned that male and female sexual attitudes and values may be more alike than different.*
12. *I feel comfortable being with a member of the opposite sex.*
13. *I am secure enough to behave the way I want even if it does not conform to the expectations of others.*
14. *I am not letting the compulsive needs of the horny stage control my behavior.*
15. *I am solving the neediness of the horny stage in a manner that is acceptable to me.*
16. *I understand and accept that many people will have no desire and may be unable to perform sexually while in deep grief.*
17. *I am getting my "quota" of hugs every week.*

RESPONSIBILITY:
Let's Treat Each Other As Adults!

Most marriages that end in divorce were out-of-balance in terms of responsibility. One partner was over-responsible, the other was under-responsible. When couples try to change this system of interaction, it is often the beginning of the end of the relationship. Feelings and attitudes within keep one operating in the under-responsible or over-responsible style; one may have to make some major changes to become adult. Equal responsibility relationships are more flexible and able to adjust to stress and change, and thus are more likely to last.

chapter fourteen

In my first marriage I took care of him.
In my second love-relationship, I let him take care of me.
Maybe next time I will be able to have an adult relationship.

Janice

Have you noticed in this climb up the mountain there are some people who seem to like to carry others, fuss over them, and help them with their lunch? They seem to be more interested in *taking care of* others and shoving them along than they are in getting up the mountain themselves. Of course it takes both kinds of people to make this work — there are others who are always wanting someone to take care of them, who do not seem to be able to make it and "need help" from someone else.

Notice also the "Marine Sergeants" ordering everyone around and acting as though they know how things should be done. They are saying "You should..." or "You ought...," critical of the way the others are climbing the trail. The people they order around and criticize tend to be either helpless and obedient or rebellious and disobedient.

I have found that 99 and 44/100 percent of the people participating in the seminars discover that they had an imbalance of responsibility in their marriages. This appears to be a major cause of marital breakdown. (Are you still keeping track?) Because the responsibility is not equal, the relationship is not flexible enough to adjust to stress and change. A team of horses pulls the load most effectively when both are pulling equally, not when one is pulling and the other is following.

Take a moment to look back at your relationship. Were you the over-responsible helper, the dominating person? Or perhaps you were the under-responsible, "helpless" or rebellious partner? If either of you tried to change this pattern, the relationship became troubled — maybe that was the beginning of the end. And the person who tried to change this rigid structure of responsibility into a more flexible adult relationship is often looked upon as the *bad-person* who upset the apple-cart. I hope you can start simply *describing* what happened instead of needing to label people as *good* and *bad* persons. Life is a process of changing and the person who instigates change may simply be a part of the life process.

If you are familiar with Transactional Analysis, you recognize that what I am talking about is similar to the terms *parent* and *child ego-states*. The parent ego state is the over-responsible part of the personality, and the child ego-state is the under-responsible part. Freud also used similar terms when he talked about the *super-ego* (the over-responsible aspect of personality) and the *id* (the under-responsible part).

The under- and over-responsible parts of personality not only come into play when we interact with others, but are important within ourselves. Most clients who come to me for counseling are having an internal war between the over- and under-responsible parts of their personalities. This internal strife is consuming much of their emotional energy and they are tired. They want the internal peace of mind they have not found. Either the over-responsible part of the personality is winning the war and they feel guilty, drained, inhibited, controlled and driven; or the under-responsible part is winning and they are impulsive, violent, irresponsible, helpless. Whichever side is winning, the losing side is continually striking back and the war goes on. Some participants in my seminars report that the major war in their marriages was not between spouses but within themselves, and the spouse was a spectator — not a partici-pant.

Not resolving this inner conflict can have serious consequences for one's relationships. In one seminar, Charlie began to introduce himself to the class, "My name is Charlie and I have been married 31 years..." At this point, he broke down and cried. Later, during the class discussion, Charlie asked if he had been the over-responsible helper in his marriage. When the participants agreed that he was, Charlie asked, "Does my being over-responsible have anything to do with her dumping me?" A woman participant stated profoundly, "Kids grow up and leave home, Charlie." This graphic description allowed Charlie to see beyond the blaming and guilt.

The vast majority of participants in my seminars call themselves over-responsible. I was puzzled by this: shouldn't there be an equal number of over- and under-responsible people taking the seminar? To find the answer, I went to work to better understand these over-responsible folks.

A close look at the two types of over-responsible persons shows that they are not just giving others a hand when it is needed to make it through a difficult time. They seem to be so busy finding people to rescue that neither the *rescuer* nor the *rescuee* makes good progress. They seem to enjoy *looking after other* persons rather than being responsible for themselves. It seems obvious that they need to get on with their own lives!

These people are great at giving to others, but have difficulty taking gifts, compliments, help from others. They learned at an early age to get their emotional kicks and rewards by taking care of others. Frank was only in junior high when his father was seriously injured. Frank took over the responsibility of the family farm and not only did the physical work but made the decisions. He became an over-responsible person, receiving recognition for how grown-up he acted. Unfortunately, even in his marriage he never was able to develop the fun-loving, "irresponsible child" part of his personality. After his divorce he was able to go through his "teenage" development, and to become a more complete whole person. Many over-responsible helping persons are nurturing others because they need to be nurtured. They learned to take care of others to compensate for their feelings of loneliness, lack of emotional nurturing, and feelings of rejection. (After all, how can you reject someone who is taking care of you?)

In her marriage, Mary was always very responsible with the money and kept a checkbook. She decided how to spend the money, even though many times Carl would criticize how much money she was spending. She usually also set the alarm clock before they went to bed, would shut it off in the morning, and always made sure Carl got up on time to make it to work. One day Mary realized she had three *other* children and she was tired of being *married* to a *child*. She began to change things so Carl had to take more responsibility, such as figuring his own checkbook, getting himself to work in the morning, and so on. Shortly after that he began an affair with another woman.

Karen was reluctant to take the seminar because she wanted "a course that would help her children." After we had discussed how the over-responsible person is a good giver but a poor taker, I asked if I could give her a hug. She jumped at the opportunity, came rushing over and gave me a hug. I backed off and pointed out that I would like to give *her* a hug. "I'll try to take a hug," she said, and stood there like a board, stiff and uncomfortable. After about two seconds, she said, "I can't stand it anymore!" and grabbed me again. Since the homework for that week was for the nurturing person to learn to *take*, I emphasized to Karen that she needed to work on her homework.

Next week she came back and shared with the group how she had worked at letting her children give to her. It was such an important change in behavior and she shed some tears while sharing it. I again asked if I could give her a hug and she said "yes," while waiting for me to come to her. I hugged her and she broke into uncontrollable sobbing and shared with the group that this was the first time she had really been able to emotionally take since she was a child. If you scratch the surface of an over-responsible helping person, you usually find a child part of that person that needs to be loved unconditionally.

Are you one of these over-responsible helping persons? If so, do you realize how easy it is for you to continue in that role when you enter into another love-relationship? As a child, Margaret liked to bring home stray cats and nurse them to good health. She grew up, brought home another "stray cat," and married him. She knew he drank a little while they were courting but she had no idea he was an alcoholic. (Most of us were so naive when we married!) She was able to leave and divorce him, but she found, after several more love-relationships, that she was continuing the same pattern. If you don't change yourself *internally*, you will probably find yourself continuing self-defeating patterns. You too could be "bringing home stray cats!"

Would you like some suggestions as to how you might change? Here is the homework that we use in the seminars to help people begin to change this pattern of giving but never taking: Part one is to say "no" next time a person asks you to do something. The over-responsible style — TA calls it "nurturing parent behavior" — is to always say "yes" to anything anyone asks you. "You can always depend on ol' Martha to do a responsible job." But saying "no" is only part of the homework. The second part of this assignment is to ask someone to do something for you. Do not pay for it, do not promise to do something in return. Don't cheat and explain that it was suggested in this book! Just ask. Are you aware of your fear of being rejected? Most of you learned to be the helping person to compensate for feelings of rejection, so this homework not only attempts to change the giving-and-never-taking style that drained you emotionally, but it also forces you to deal with the possibility of rejection.

The more extreme you are in this helping role, the more difficult this homework will be for you. I can almost hear some of you exclaim, "I can't ask anyone to do something for me!" I have many participants in the class say those words. My response is: "Some of you may not be strong enough to change at this time. Maybe you'll be able to even if you think you can't. Give it a try, maybe it will be easier than you think."

Some people hold the sexist view that it is only females that become over-responsible helping persons. I believe that our society does encourage women to play the helping role — saying in many ways that "a woman's role is to help and support her husband." But in my seminars males are just as often over-responsible helpers, so it appears that development of the over-responsible helping person-ality has to do with other factors than whether you were born male or female.

Let's look again at my puzzlement about why so many partici-pants of the seminars are helping people. One likely answer is that they are continuing the pattern of being over-responsible; they take the seminar because that would be a responsible thing to do. But underneath I believe there is another need operating. Because the seminar is emotionally warm and supportive, people take the seminar to *get* the nurturing they need. The past pattern of inter-action leaves them feeling emotionally drained and hungry for nur-turing. It appears that one step toward overcoming the pattern of

parental, over-responsible helper is to become an under-responsible
taking child for a time. Filling our own needs helps us to become
balanced, which leads us to adultness and to equal responsibility in
our next love-relationships.

What is the difference between over-responsible helping persons
and those spiritually concerned people who are caring and concerned about others? I use the classic "fish story" to illustrate the
difference. One way to help a hungry person is for the rescuer to
give him or her a fish. The next day the hungry person comes again
and the rescuer gives another fish. Pretty soon the hungry one is
"hooked" (the person — not the fish). An *adult* helper teaches the
hungry person to fish. The *rescuer* has a need to take care of others
so giving the fish meets his or her needs more than it does the
hungry person. The *adult* becomes the teacher and finds satisfaction
from seeing the other person learn to meet his or her own needs.

Let's switch now to the other type of over-responsible person —
the critical and domineering "Marine Sergeant." Barb told the
seminar that she always felt little and helpless with her husband.
When she started to stick up for herself and not give in to Sam's
domination, the marriage began to crumble. Barb felt guilty —
"like the bad person" — but the group helped her see that it is
better to simply describe change and how it affects the relationship,
rather than labeling people good or bad.

Barb has trouble understanding why Sam is having such a difficult time adjusting to single life. He keeps coming back to her like a
lost puppy dog searching for his master. "He dominated me all the
time — why does he appear to be so lost and needy?" Can you
imagine, Barb, how the Marine Sergeant would feel if the platoon of
recruits that he has been ordering around were all suddenly gone?

Over-responsible persons, whether the helping or dominating
type, need someone to take care of as part of their identity. It is as
though they have to be carried on the shoulders of another person in
order to be tall. When it happens that submissive persons leave
their old love-relationships — either physically or emotionally — the
dominating partners crumble like a house of playing cards. They
easily become vulnerable because they are so fragile.

Let me ask those of you who have been domineering and critical partners, "Which one of your parents was a perfectionist?" Most of you will answer, "Both of them were perfectionists." We learn to be critical of others from those who are critical of us. We keep striving to be perfect because that was what our parents kept expecting of us.

Have you thought about how difficult it is to be perfect? How hard you strive to please? How hard you are on yourself? Those years of criticism in childhood are bound to result in some insecure, anxious, fearful feelings. Many people compensate for these feelings by striving to be perfect in order to feel loved. Others push those close to them to "do better," through criticism and never-satisfied demands.

The alcoholic personality has a large part that is self-critical. Drinking first diminishes the power of the parental and critical part of the personality, then the rational, adult part, then the fun loving child part, and finally results in unconsciousness. Many alcoholics drink enough to diminish the critical part of the personality; that is an important cause of their drinking, allowing the "child inside" to have fun. Wouldn't it be nice to learn to have fun and be ourselves without having to drink to do it?

Here's some homework that has proven to be effective for partici-pants in the seminars. If what you are really trying to do is to become perfect, realize that no one can be perfect, and stop trying. Next week, stop all the compulsive behavior that you have felt you had to do. A good example for most critical persons: stop making your bed every morning. "Oh, I can't do that. I can't leave that room without making the bed. The room looks so messy. I'd sooner be late to work or to church than to leave the room messy." Think about what your compulsive behavior is. What is it that you think you *have* to do every day? Is it really "critically" important to your life? George, a member of one class, started thinking about that and he adopted a new motto for life while adjusting to his divorce — *it doesn't matter*. Try it and see if that motto will help you to let go of the critical part of your personality. Letting go of the parental and critical part of our personalities, we have to become somewhat irresponsible in an almost childlike way. Many people have to go through a "childish" stage in order to leave the parental and reach adulthood.

Since over-responsible persons need to learn to take responsibility for their own behavior instead of that of others, they find this homework assignment helpful: whenever you notice someone close to you is acting rebellious, monitor your own behavior and determine if *you* are setting this up with your style of interaction.

I mentioned earlier that there are relatively few of the "under-responsible" type persons in my seminars. Usually these folks learned at an early age that all they had to do was to play helpless and someone would take care of them. Typical vocabulary is "I don't know how," "I need someone to teach me," "I feel so frightened that I can't do it." These people have trouble balancing their checkbooks, seldom if ever make their beds, always leave decisions up to the over-responsible person. Some of them — those who *really believe* they are helpless — have so little confidence in their capacities that they are unwilling to *try* to be self-sufficient. The rebellious ones, on the other hand, go through life intentionally irresponsible and carefree, and if something goes wrong they take no responsibility: "It's *your* fault!"

It is easy for me to give under-responsible people some homework, but they either comply, which leaves the responsibility upon me, or are under-responsible and do not do the homework — rationalizing that it was too hard. So my suggestion for you under-responsible folks is to figure out *your own* homework. If you really want to change, you will find ways of becoming more responsible. And I will listen to your behavior rather than your words. I have heard the words many times.

Isn't it interesting: to change any behavior, the person first has to become responsible for her or his own behavior. It is often believed that the over-responsible person, with a more parental behavior style, is somehow more mature. Under- and over-responsible behavior are both immature, and there is little difference between the two in this respect. Maturity is a process of becoming more responsible for one's own behavior; adultness is a state of assuming responsibility in a mature manner.

Incidentally, an important goal is to allow ourselves *flexibility* in taking responsibility. When we come home tired from a difficult day at work, it is appropriate to allow ourselves the luxury of being cared for. (The over-responsible person becomes more so when tired; and the under-responsible person becomes more that way when tired.) So allow someone to bring you a drink, to hold you, to listen to you share your troubles of the day. On the other hand you may become over-responsible when another is sick, when one has a need to "play little," to be cared for. With flexibility, you can adjust and function at an appropriate level of responsibility. This flexibility is adultness; you choose the type of interaction rather than allowing it to choose you. You are flexible within yourself as to how responsible you are in a situation, and you are also flexible in your interactions with others. This flexibility allows the adult relationship to adjust to change and stress that occurs as part of the process of life.

Here is a brief exercise which may help you to more fully understand these different types of interactions, so that you may monitor your own growth toward adultness. As you read through the six situations, note that each has three different responses; illustrating over- and under-responsible, and adult behavior. There is no "score" for this exercise; simply note the way each style shows itself in everyday situations.

1. The single mother is leaving on a date. Her oldest daughter's farewell comment is:
        A. "Be sure to get home early tonight, Mum."
        B. "I'd like a phone number where I can reach you if I need to."
        C. "Wow, kids, will we have fun tonight while Mum is gone!"

2. The wife makes these comments after she has been informed by her husband that he wants a divorce:
        A. "I never was good enough for you."
        B. "Maybe we should discuss our problem with a marriage counselor."
        C. "You should learn to take responsibility for your life instead of running away like a child."

3. Your son, age 13, says, "You're without a doubt the worst parent a kid like me could ever have." You respond:
    A. "I can see that you're very angry with me and wish that I would act differently."
    B. "I've done everything I could possibly do for you; about time you grew up!"
    C. "So — big deal! Who cares?"

4. The minister's sermon on Mothers' Day talks only about two-parent families. You are a single mother and your response is:
    A. "I'm never going to go to that church again."
    B. "Doesn't that minister know that the whole world is becoming divorced nowadays?"
    C. "I'm going to call the minister this week and explain to him how I felt about the sermon."

5. The woman asks for an unreasonable property settlement, and the man's response is:
    A. "I'm going to hire the meanest lawyer in town to teach you a lesson."
    B. "I think we should talk to a third party to help mediate this dispute."
    C. "I'm tired of fighting. You can have everything you want."

6. A noncustodial father has taken the children to visit him while his new girl friend is present, and the mother's response is:
    A. "You chose to be with that woman instead of me, so my children are never going to be around you while she's there."
    B. "Do you think I want my children seeing their father acting like a teenager?"
    C. "Our children will need a lot of time and attention from you while they're visiting you. Will you be able to give them the quality time they need while your girl friend is present?"

Many times in ending your love-relationship you did not respond at an adult level with your former love-partner. While you are ending the relationship, I strongly suggest that you try to remain as adult as possible when talking and communicating with your ex. It will be easy for him or her to hook you into being under- or over-responsible, with resulting arguments and bad feelings. Communication between the two of you is enhanced if you can have adult interactions, and it is valuable practice for other relationships as well!

We have discussed in this chapter how much of our over- and under-responsible behavior was learned in our childhood. What kind of behavior are you teaching your **children**? If your children have not had first-hand exposure to adult relationships in the family interaction as they grow up, it will be difficult for them to do it in their own marriages. One of the greatest things we can do for our kids is to develop an increasingly adult relationship with them as they grow.

Awareness, understanding, and knowledge leads us to more adultness both in our behavior with others and within ourselves. What you have learned in this chapter can help you to become more adult. Here is a check list for you to evaluate your development of more adult behavior.

1. *I can identify my behavior as to over- and under-responsibility, and adultness.*
2. *I can see the over- and under-responsible behavior in my past love-relationship, both in myself and in my partner.*
3. *I believe that past patterns of interaction can be changed.*
4. *I am doing the homework suggested to change my behavior toward more adultness.*
5. *I am building adult relationships at this time.*
6. *I am allowing myself flexibility, to behave with whatever responsibility is appropriate.*
7. *I expect to continue to build adult relationships in the future.*

SINGLENESS: You Mean It's Okay?

In the singleness stage, you emphasize investment in your own personal growth rather than in other relationships. A period of singleness enables you to build confidence in yourself so you can experience and enjoy being single as an acceptable alternative lifestyle, not as a time to be lonely. It is easy, however, to become stuck in this rebuilding block as a means of avoiding another intimate love-relationship.

chapter fifteen

I've become aware that living as a single person is an affirmation of strength and self — not an embarrassing admission of failure.

I'm more relaxed in the company of others — I no longer am wasting emotional energy being a social chameleon.

Post-marital guilt, self-doubts, and questions like "Will I ever love again?" are greatly diminished.

I am happy as a single person — something I had not thought possible before.

Larry

Have you ever been on a hike when someone in the hiking party decided to walk on by themselves instead of staying with the group? They want to be by themselves and with their own thoughts, and to enjoy the view alone. You will notice several people walking by themselves during this part of the climb. They have gained enough confidence in their climbing ability that they choose to walk at their own pace, rather than following the crowd. They choose time to be alone as a way of investing in themselves. I call it the singleness stage.

Many people never learned to be single persons before they married. They went from parental homes to marriage homes, never even considered that one could be happy living as a single person, and never questioned the myth that one became married and lived happily ever after.

Mona lived with her parents until she married Joe. She went from pleasing one man, her father, to pleasing another man, her husband. When Joe first talked about leaving, she clung to him because the thought of living alone was terrifying. She had never learned to please herself. She had always been a dependent person; and now the thought of being independent, although challenging, was frightening to her. She was embarrassed because it really sounded silly to her that a woman of 25 did not know her own mind, or know what to do with her life.

Gradually she adjusted to being alone. At first she searched for other relationships, something/someone to lean on. As she became more and more confident, she began doing more things for herself and enjoying it. She wallpapered a whole bedroom; sawed the boards and pounded the nails for a new patio fence; went to a movie by herself one afternoon while the kids were with Joe; and even enjoyed stumbling alone in the dark trying to find a seat. She invited the whole neighborhood in for a party. These activities left her feeling exhilarated, knowing that she did not need anyone. She was a good example of a woman becoming liberated.

Jim represents the male side of this same coin. He had been well cared for by his mother. The clothes were always washed and ironed, meals were on time, and even his room was kept clean. He could devote his time to school, school activities, and his job. When he entered college, he lived in a dorm. Again his meals were provided and he had a minimum of housekeeping chores. Then he married and Janet did all the things that his mother had always done. He felt independent and did not realize how dependent he actually was. But he found out when he left Janet. He was helpless in the kitchen, even in preparing the simplest meal. He had very little understanding of how to wash his clothes, and ended up with pink underwear when he put them in the wash with colored socks! You can pay for car maintenance, but it is difficult — and very expensive — to hire a full-time cook and housekeeper.

Gradually Jim's self-prepared meals improved. Finally he got brave enough to invite a female friend to his home to eat, and she was delighted with the meal he prepared. His clothes began to look more cared for. He was very pleased and proud when he learned to iron his own shirts! He felt that learning to care for himself was like growing up — each accomplishment left a feeling of success and achievement.

But the singleness I am talking about is much more than learning to do the tasks that someone else has done for you. It is a whole way of life. Dating and love-relationships are a good example. A typical comment from a recently separated person might be, "I'll never make it as a single person; I need another love-relationship." During the singleness stage, the same person might say, "Why get remarried? I can come and go as I please. I can eat whenever I feel like it. I don't have to adjust my daily living habits to another person. Being single sure feels good!''

Before the singleness stage, one may be looking for the ''lost half.'' But during this stage one reaches the point of comfort in going out alone. No longer is a ''date'' necessary to avoid embarrassment or a feeling of failure. The quality of relationships improves, since one now *chooses* whom to go out with rather than taking whoever seems available. And the whole evening out may be spent *sharing* rather than *needing*. Other persons may be encountered and enjoyed for who they are, rather than as potential life-time companions.

One of the homework assignments in our seminars has to do with developing new interests in the singleness stage. Many have spent their free, recreational time in the past doing what the spouse wanted or what they had learned to do with their parents. The assignment is simply to take the time to develop a new interest, or to pursue something that one may have wanted to do for a long time. It might be to learn to play the guitar, to paint, to drive a car, or to play a new sport. Participants find many new activities that *they* really enjoy — not what someone else always enjoyed.

In the last chapter I discussed adult responsibility and parent-child behavior. Perhaps you see how the singleness stage allows us to change these roles. Because the roles we act out in our relationships are so closely related to our internal attitudes and feelings, we change inside as we change our external roles. It is easier to do this in the singleness stage than when we are in permanent love-relationships. A *neutral environment* facilitates both internal and external changes. The singleness stage is a key period to make the internal changes in attitudes and feelings necessary for personal growth.

Parenting is different during the singleness stage. In earlier stages parents frequently bend themselves out of shape trying to make sure they are lovable, datable, and okay in many other ways. The kids often suffer; their needs are put on the ''back-burner.'' In the singleness stage, parents usually are more responsive to the needs of the kids. Susannah had been volunteering in the seminars because she ''needed'' to feel worthwhile by helping others. When she began to reach the singleness stage, she resigned as a volunteer because she wanted to spend more time with her children. Parents in the singleness stage have begun to rise above their own emotional needs.

Not everything is rosy in the singleness stage, of course. Research shows that single people may still not fare as well economically. Single persons are passed over for promotions, looked upon as fair game romantically and sexually, and may — particularly single women — even be asked for "favors" in order to be promoted. The tax laws favor married couples who may file income tax jointly. Big changes have been made in obtaining credit for single people; nevertheless, there remain many forms of economic discrimination against singles.

There are other situations that make single people feel uncomfortable. Alexa complained about her child's Sunday School class. When the teacher asked the children to draw pictures of their families, Alexa's son drew a picture of himself, his sister, and his mother — which was his family. The teacher made him draw a picture of a man in the family because, "We all know that a family consists of both a father and a mother!" Alexa expressed her negative feelings by talking directly with the minister of the church.

Ursula went to church on Mother's Day and the sermon was about marital love. Although she was a mother, she felt completely left out of the sermon. It was a depressing day in church for her. She wrote a letter to the minister explaining her feelings.

Schools are often an irritating problem when you are a single parent. The PTA chairperson calls and asks that Johnny's parents run the dart show. The single-parent father explains that he is single but would be willing to come alone. The chairperson informs him that it takes two to run the show and she will ask someone else to handle it. PTA meetings themselves are often couple-oriented; you can feel really single and alone when you attend without a partner.

You come alone to a parent-teacher conference, and the teacher informs you that "all of the *problem children* in the room have just one parent," and that is why she wanted to see you. Your child may not be getting "the parenting she needs," and perhaps that is why she is doing so poorly in her school work. What's more, your daughter is "so boy crazy for a sixth grader!" It is implied that if

Mom had a ''permanent'' relationship with one man, Janie would have a better attitude toward males. You feel angry, vulnerable, and defenseless. What can you say?

It often takes a great deal of inner security to handle the singleness stage successfully. Much of the discussion in this chapter concerns the internal feelings present in the singleness stage. If you have worked your way through the prior rebuilding blocks, it is likely that you will be able to experience the peacefulness and calmness that occurs in the singleness stage. You may become slightly upset about the attitudes of others, but you will be strong enough to handle them. Learn from the external prejudices and use them to become more secure in your own internal feelings. Develop some assertive responses for the most common put-downs and discriminatory acts. You can help to educate others, while maintaining your own integrity, by responding firmly. You will feel better inside, too, rather than going away fuming!

Singleness can be one of the most productive stages you go through in the climb, in the sense that the old wounds can really be healed. Dealing with the external discrimination may help you to become stronger inside.

The singleness stage is an easy stage in which to become stuck. If you have not worked through all of the leftovers concerning marriage and intimacy, you may use the singleness stage as a place to hide. It may sound like the singleness stage when you hear someone say, ''I'll never marry again.'' But in many ways that is the opposite of genuine singleness. Fear of intimacy, avoidance of feelings, and opposition to marriage as though it were the worst institution in our society — all indicate that the person is *stuck*. The goal is to be *free to choose* singleness or remarriage, not to stay single forever.

Singleness has become an acceptable alternative in our society. When I was a child, a single person was looked upon in our community as somewhat weird, one who just did not quite make it to the altar. It was patriotic to be married because, after all, the family was the cornerstone of our society. Attitudes are changing; at a talk I gave on love-relationships the other night, a woman wanted to know why we had to keep talking about *relationships*. Was not it just as valid to talk about remaining single? Did we have to keep looking toward being in a relationship as the ideal? The fact that there are approximately a million divorces in the United States each year makes singleness more acceptable for many. The large number of formerly married people in our society has brought about many changes in attitudes toward singleness. Perhaps we are becoming more accepting of individual differences? Let us hope so!

Singleness is an important rebuilding block for **children**, too. They need to learn to be single, individual, independent-from-parents people before they marry for the first time. If children can see and understand the importance of singleness, it will give them a much better chance to develop successful love-relationships in their future.

At this point, the climb up the mountain has the big advantage of a view above the timberline. You can see forever. And the single-ness stage is definitely above the timberline. You can see the real world much better. You can know yourself much better. You understand people and the interactions with people much better. Your viewpoint of life is much broader. Down in the plains before the crisis occurred, your vision was limited. Now you see and understand concepts never before understood. The singleness stage is almost to the top. Let's hurry and see the view from that peak!

Here are some items to check yourself with before the final climb.

1. *I am comfortable being single.*
2. *I can be happy as a single person.*
3. *I am comfortable going to social events as a single person.*
4. *I see being single as an acceptable alternative lifestyle.*
5. *I am becoming a whole person rather than a half-person looking for my other lost half.*
6. *I am spending time investing in my own personal growth rather than looking for another love-relationship.*
7. *I can look at my friends as people I want to be with rather than as potential love-partners.*
8. *If I have children and family, I can spend time enjoying being with them rather than begrudging the time they take from my personal life.*
9. *I have found internal peace and contentment as a single person.*

FREEDOM: From Chrysalis to Butterfly

By working through the rebuilding blocks, you can build more meaningful relationships in your future. You will have the freedom to choose to be free and happy either as a single person or in another love-relationship. Freedom is being able to be fully yourself.

chapter sixteen

I felt many times in my marriage that I was trapped in a prison of love. It was hard to be myself when there were so many demands and expectations placed upon me. When I first separated, I felt even worse. But now I have found that I can fly. I can be me. I feel like I left the chrysalis and have become a butterfly. I feel so free.

Alice

Wow! Would you look at that view from here on top of the mountain! After this paragraph, I want you to stop reading for a moment and take time to go on a fantasy trip. Imagine being on top of a mountain with a view of other peaks and valleys below. Smell the pine trees; let the clear, bright high-altitude sun warm your skin. Notice the clouds lower than you are, and feel the cool breeze blowing off the snow glaciers. Notice how far away the horizon is out over the plains, and how far you can see. Think back about the climb. What was the most enjoyable and interesting portion for you? What was the most difficult part? The most painful? Can you identify the many changes that have taken place within you? Have you really reached the top emotionally or are you only at the top in your mind? Think about how it feels at the top, having worked so hard in your climb of personal growth. Take as much time as you want with this fantasy before you go on reading.

When you have thought about your fantasy carefully, turn the page and continue reading.

On the singleness portion of the trail, I hope you found not only that it feels good to be single, but that it may be the most productive behavior for you during the climb. Now you need to think about what working your way through these rebuilding blocks has done to the way you interact with those around you. The way you react to loneliness, grief, rejection, guilt, anger, and love significantly determines how you handle your daily life and your interactions with others. Many divorced people have had considerable difficulty with one or more of the rebuilding blocks. If you really work at the rebuilding process, overcoming each stumbling block, then you will be able to enter into another love-relationship and make it more productive than the last one. You will be able to meet your own needs and the needs of your loved one(s) much better than in the past. Rebuilding not only helps you to survive the crisis, but it also enhances your future love-relationships. That feels good!

Perhaps you were widowed and were satisfied with the happiness you felt in your last relationship. Research indicates that people who were widowed have remarriages which are more likely to last. Being widowed is a painful and very difficult adjustment process, and most of the rebuilding blocks are helpful to those who are going through that crisis. Many widowed persons, however, do not have one of the toughest parts of the adjustment — that of dealing with the previous, unhappy love-relationship.

For many people, the climb is so difficult that they feel like quitting before reaching the top. I have heard countless people say, "I want to stop climbing and take a rest! I'm tired of growing." And many do stop along the way because they are tired, frightened, or feel unable to handle the change. My response is the same I would offer to someone who gets tired on a hike: sit and rest; get your energy back; then *keep on climbing* because the view at the top is worth it. I find that support, hope, and a belief that you can make it are helpful. But it is up to you in the end. Probably the best evidence of the difficulty of the climb comes from the small percentage of people at the top. Do you have the self-discipline, desire, courage, and stamina to make it?

Now comes the "truth in packaging" disclaimer: I cannot *promise* that you will be happier, or wealthier, or more fulfilled if you complete the climb. I can assure you that there are few turkeys and more eagles at this altitude, but I cannot promise that you will find an eagle for yourself (except when you look in the mirror!). The plain hard fact is that you will not *necessarily* find another "just right" person with whom to create a lasting relationship. What you will find is that you like yourself better, you can enjoy being alone and single, and the people whom you meet up here will be pretty special — after all, they made this tough climb, too!

It is true that there are fewer persons here from which to choose. An awful lot of folks just did not make it this far — indeed, many are still at the base camp, playing social games, hiding behind emotional walls, and finding excuses not to undertake the climb. The lack of numbers here may make the process of finding new friends and potential lovers more difficult. But I have found that the relationships with others at the top have such a higher quality that quantity is not so important. When you are really at the top, giving off those good vibrations, there are many people attracted to you. I do not think the top of the mountain is as lonely as parts of the trail were on the way up. And if you are still feeling lonely, maybe you have not reached the top emotionally.

You may get discouraged at times when you realize that the old patterns have crept back and you really have not changed as much as you thought. Do you normally put on your right or left shoe first? Try to reverse your routine this next week and put on the other shoe first. I will bet you forget and go back to the old ways. It is difficult to make changes in your daily living habits, and even harder to make changes in your personality. Keep up your determination and you will make it. Do not get discouraged — it may come slowly!

You may greatly fear the unknown future. You are not alone! It may be learning to be single; it may be not knowing what to expect or what is expected of you. How do you feel the first time you drive or ride in a new city that is unfamiliar to you? Confused, lost, uncertain? How about the way you feel the first time you go to a singles party? There is a certain amount of comfort in the known. Your old relationship may look good even if it was like living in hell. I hope that if you go back to the old relationship, it will be for more positive reasons than fear of the unknown future!

I have talked a great deal during this climb up the mountain about the importance of learning to be single. Let me get in a last word about the importance of relationships. We can become whole by emotionally working hard at becoming whole. But I believe there is a part of each of us that needs another person to help us become completely fulfilled. A love-relationship is more than icing on the cake, but that analogy seems to fit: the cake is whole without icing, but ever so much *sweeter* with it! I think each of us needs another person to help us become completely fulfilled, and to make life sweeter!

When you were in the pits of the crisis, you gave no thought to plans and goals for the future. Part of your grief was concerned with loss of future, since you had to give up the plans and goals you had in that love-relationship. But when you came out of the pits, you began looking to the future and making plans again. Ernie, a member of one of my seminars who works in a hospital, told the group one evening, "It's like the process in the hospital psych wards. There's a crafts room where the patients spend time. When patients first are admitted, they have no energy to work on crafts. But when they begin to be really interested in crafts, this is a good indication that they're ready to be discharged. I felt ready to be discharged from the divorce pits when I started making plans for the future!"

My research has found that recently separated people, and especially dumpees, are very much "living in the past," thinking mostly about how it "used to be." Further along in the process, people stop living in the past and start living in the present, enjoying the sunsets. I hope by now you have stopped living in the past, and are living in the present and making plans for your own future.

Recently separated people, and again especially dumpees, are very dependent upon others, according to my research. As people grow further in the process, they gain more independence, and find a good balance between independence and dependence. Have you found a good balance between dependence and independence?

Children need to work their way through the rebuilding blocks, and to learn the freedom to be themselves, free from all the unhealthy needs that control so many people. They need to be free to choose marriage. Quite frequently children of divorce say that they will not get married because they saw how devastating divorce was to their parents. Children need freedom of choice in what they will do with their lives, rather than to follow or contradict their parents' pattern.

All children are not the same, nor do they have the same needs. I have been generalizing a great deal about children, in reference to each of the rebuilding blocks. Remember that they are each a unique human being, and that it is as important for them as it is for adults that they be respected and treated as such! Their differing needs depend upon age, sex, cultural background, number of children in the family, health, availability of extended family and/or friends and neighbors, physical environment, conditions at school, and the nature of their parents' breakup, as well as the individual personal characteristics of each child.

Kids are stronger than you think, and can grow through the rebuilding process right along with you. I encourage you to help them do so!

I thought you might like a self-evaluation report card to help you see how you are doing in your personal growth. You may wish to check yourself now and occasionally in the future, say once a month, or at least in two months, six months, a year. The list includes some important aspects of personal growth that you need to be aware of in order to keep growing. Most of these are areas I have talked about as we climbed the mountain, and you may want to go back and review them in the book.

"How Am I Doing?"

1. *I am able to put into words what I am feeling.*
2. *I am able to communicate to another person what I am feeling.*
3. *I have at least one life-line friend of each sex that I can ask for help when I feel I am drowning in the river of life.*
4. *I can express my anger in a positive manner that is not destructive to me or to those around me.*
5. *I am keeping a journal of my feelings and attitudes as I adjust to my crisis.*
6. *I have made at least one new friend, or renewed an old friendship in the past month.*

7. I have invested quality time with at least one friend this past week.

8. I have identified which of the rebuilding blocks I need to work on, and have made a plan to start my further work.

9. I have invested time into a growing experience such as reading a good book, taking an educational class, attending an interesting lecture, or watching an educational program on TV this past week.

10. I have seriously considered if I would benefit from a therapy relationship in order to enhance my personal growth or to speed up my adjustment process.

11. I have received my quota of hugs from my friends this week.

12. I have spent time by myself either in prayer, meditation, or solitary thought this past week.

13. I have nurtured myself with a kind deed this past week.

14. I listen to the aches, tensions, and feelings in my body to learn more about myself.

15. I exercise regularly.

16. I have made at least one change in my daily living habits that I feel good about this past week.

17. I nourish my body with an adequate diet.

18. I have given emotionally of myself to at least one friend this past week.

19. I have invested in my spiritual growth this past week.

20. I like being the person I am.

21. I am making plans for my future.

22. I have let the "natural child" within me have fun this past week.

23. I am not carrying around pent up feelings of anger, grief, loneliness, rejection, or guilt but have learned to express them in order to rid myself of them.

24. I am much more in control of my life than I was when my past love-relationship ended.

25. I am experiencing the feeling of freedom to be myself.

26. I am actively using the concepts learned from this book to help speed up my adjustment process.

Well, how *are* you doing? Are you satisfied with your self-evaluuative "report card?" I hope it will also help to summarize some of the important concepts that we have talked about in this climb.

What is this freedom we all seem to be striving for? Freedom is something you find inside you. And you find it by becoming free from unmet needs which control you, such as the need to avoid being alone, the need to feel guilty, the need to find a critical parent to please, or the need to get free from your own "parent within you."

The butterfly at the top of the mountain stands for the freedom you find to fly and land where you choose. You can be free from the bonds that have kept you from being the person you would like to be. The person you were meant to be. The person you are capable of being. Our worst enemies are those within us, and it is those demons from which we need to free ourselves.

Climbing the mountain not only gives us the freedom of choice to seek happiness either alone or in another love-relationship — it also gives us the freedom to be ourselves. And that makes the climb of personal growth worthwhile.

It is tough for me to end this book, because I know it represents just a *beginning* for you. I have watched hundreds of people go through the rebuilding process. They have taught me a great deal. You could help me learn more by dropping me a note, in care of my publisher, to let me know how *REBUILDING* has helped you, and how I could make it even better.

I hope you will not put this book away on a shelf, but that you will *use* it, as often as you need to, as a tool to help you rebuild. Share it with a friend, or perhaps give your friend his or her own copy.

Most of all — I wish you success in your continuing personal growth.

196

footnotes

1. The Fisher Divorce Adjustment Scale is a 100-item standardized measure of how people have adjusted to the end of their love-relationships. Considerable research has been conducted with the Scale, and most who take it find the results very useful. For further information, see Appendix.

2. Alberti, R.E. and Emmons, M.L., **Your Perfect Right: A Guide to Assertive Behavior** (Third edition). San Luis Obispo, California: Impact Publishers, 1978.

3. Saul, S., "Effects of Grief and Personal Adjustment on Remarriage." Unpublished Doctoral Dissertation, University of Oklahoma, 1979.

appendix

THE FISHER DIVORCE ADJUSTMENT SCALE

The *Fisher Divorce Adjustment Scale* (*FDAS*) is a 100-item paper-and-pencil personality scale designed to measure how people have adjusted to the ending of their love-relationship. Several research projects have evaluated the *FDAS*, and there is now a considerable body of data which demonstrates its statistical validity and reliability.

People who have used the *FDAS* have enjoyed answering the questions (many of which are included or adapted in the check lists at the end of each chapter of *REBUILDING*), and have found it a valuable learning experience. Participants in the author's 10-week divorce and personal growth seminars complete the *FDAS* before the seminar starts, and again after the seminar. The results give them help in planning their work in the seminar, and an assessment of their growth after the 10 weeks.

Individuals who would like to complete the *FDAS* and receive a formal ''scoring'' of their results are advised to contact a marriage counselor or psychologist. The professional person may arrange to purchase the *FDAS* (see address below), arrange for scoring, and be available for consultation on results.

Further information is available from:

> Family Relations Learning Center
> 450 Ord Drive
> Boulder, Colorado 80303

bibliography

*Indicates books that participants in the Divorce and Personal Growth Seminars have found helpful.

Anger

Madow, Leo. *Anger: How to Recognize and Cope with It.* New York: Charles Scribner's Sons, 1974. A traditional view of how to understand and deal with anger.

*Rubin, Theodore Isaac. *The Angry Book.* New York: Collier, 1969. One of the best books for understanding and dealing with anger effectively.

Assertiveness

Alberti, Robert & Emmons, Michael. *Your Perfect Right.* San Luis Obispo, Calif.: Impact Publishers, Inc., 1978 (third edition). A step-by-step guide to assertive behavior.

Bach, George & Goldberg, Herb. *Creative Aggression.* Garden City: Doubleday, 1974. Dedicated to those who refuse to pay the price of being nice. ••

Children of Divorce

Despert, J. Louise. *Children of Divorce.* New York: Doubleday, 1953. A classic written by a child psychiatrist.

*Gardner, Richard. *The Boys and Girls Book about Divorce.* New York: Science House, Inc., 1970. Excellent book, written at the junior high school reading level so many kids can read the book themselves. Hopefully you and your children will read it together. ••

———. *The Parents Book about Divorce.* New York: Doubleday, 1977. Dr. Gardner continues his fine work with another book for parents. ••

Gordon, Thomas. *Parent Effectiveness Training.* New York: Peter H. Wyden, Inc., 1970. This book on parenting is especially helpful for single parents of divorced children.

Magid, Ken & Schreibman, Walt. *Divorce Is...* Evergreen, Colo.: Evergreen Consultants Press, 1980.

Pomeroy, Wardell B. *Boys and Sex. Girls and Sex.* New York: Delacourt, 1968, 1969. Explicit books to explain sex to children from junior high school on. You parents may learn something, also.

Richards & Willis. *How to Get It Together When Your Parents Are Coming Apart.* New York: Bantam, 1977. Excellent for adolescents.

Salk, Lee. *What Every Child Would Like Parents to Know about Divorce.* New York: Harper & Row, 1978. Dr. Salk is one of the best-known child psychologists, and has written a useful book about children of divorce.

Sinberg, Janet. *Divorce Is a Grown Up Problem.* New York: Avon, 1978. An excellent book for elementary children.

The Divorce Process

*Colgrove, Bloomfield, & McWilliams. *How to Survive the Loss of a Love.* New York: Leo Press, 1976. This book is highly recommended for those in divorce pain. **

Fisher, Bruce. *Identifying and Meeting Needs of Formerly Married People Through a Divorce Adjustment Seminar.* Doctoral dissertation available from the Family Relations Learning Center, Boulder, Colorado, 1976. Research using the *Fisher Divorce Adjustment Scale.*

——— . "Rebuilding Blocks in the Divorce Process," *Journal of Extension,* Vol. XV, May/June, 1977.

Fisher, Esther Oshiver. *Divorce: The New Freedom.* New York: Harper & Row, 1974. A professional book by the editor of the *Journal of Divorce.*

Fuller, Jan. *Space: The Scrapbook of My Divorce.* Connecticut: Fawcett, 1973. A lovely book written by a woman as she was going through her divorce process.

Hirsch, Barbara. *Divorce: What a Woman Needs to Know.* Chicago: Henry Regnery Co., 1973. A woman lawyer writes about legal and other aspects of divorce.

Hoffman, Bob. *Getting Divorced from Mom & Dad.* Toronto: Clarke, Irwin & Co., 1976. Many people are reworking their parental relationships in their love-relationships.

Hunt, Morton M. *The World of the Formerly-Married.* New York: McGraw-Hill, 1969. One of the best books on the formerly-married subculture.

Hunt & Hunt. *The Divorce Experience: A New Look at the World of the Formerly-Married.* New York: McGraw-Hill, 1977. A comprehensive look at the formerly-married and their remarriages.

Kessler, Sheila. *The American Way of Divorce: Prescriptions for Change.* Chicago: Nelson-Hall, 1975. A helpful book by a woman who has worked with many people going through the divorce process.

*Krantzler, Melvin. *Creative Divorce.* New York: M. Evans and Co., Inc., 1974. The bestseller that tells how to make the divorce process into a creative experience. **

Moffett & Sherer. *Dealing with Divorce.* Boston: Little, Brown & Co., 1976. A practical book written from a lawyer's viewpoint.

Robertson, Christina. *Divorce and Decision Making, A Woman's Guide.* Chicago: Follett, 1980.

*Smoke, Jim. *Growing Through Divorce.* Irvine, Calif.: Harvest House, 1976. Reverend Smoke, Garden City, California, is known nationally for his ministry to singles.

Weiss, Robert S. *Marital Separation.* New York: Basic Books, Inc., 1975. A sociologist writes from his experiences working with groups for separated people.

Inspirational

Gibran, Kahlil. *The Prophet*. New York: Alfred A. Knopf, 1923. This book belongs in every home library.

Letting Go

Phillips, Debora & Judd, Robert. *How to Fall Out of Love*. Boston: Houghton Mifflin, 1978. **

Wanderer, Zev & Cabot, Tracy. *Letting Go*. East Rutherford, New Jersey: G. P. Putnam's Sons, 1978.

Loneliness

Moustakas, Clark. *Loneliness*. New Jersey: Prentice Hall, Inc., 1961. The author explains how to use loneliness to gain deeper insight into the human condition.

_____. *Loneliness and Love*. New Jersey: Prentice Hall, Inc., 1972. We need both loneliness and love for optimum personal growth.

Love

Buscaglia, Leo. *Love*. New Jersey: Charles B. Slack, Inc., 1972 (paperback: Fawcett, 1978). The "Love Doctor" from the University of Southern California talks about his favorite subject — love.**

*Fromm, Erich. *The Art of Loving*. New York: Harper & Row, Inc., 1956. A classic explaining the process of loving in a profound manner.

Hodge, Marshall Bryant. *Your Fear of Love*. Garden City: Doubleday, 1967. A practical book on how to overcome one of our most basic fears, the fear of love.

*Newman & Berhowitz. *How to be Your Own Best Friend*. New York: Random, 1971. A sensible book on giving up your childhood misconceptions and becoming your own best friend.**

Relationships

Austin, R.B. *How to Make It with Another Person*. New York: Macmillan, 1976. "Nature has built into us what it takes to enjoy intimacy, and the psychological sciences have given us the tools to use these inborn sources," says Dr. Austin.

*Bach & Deutsch. *Pairing*. New York: Peter H. Wyden, Inc., 1970. A superb book about building genuine intimate relationships. **

Bach & Wyden. *The Intimate Enemy*. New York: William Morrow, 1968. The classic on Fair-Fighting. It takes two to fair-fight and most divorced people are not able to learn to fair-fight while they are in the divorce process. **

Edwards & Hoover. *The Challenge of Being Single*. New York: Tarcher-Hawthorne, 1974. The authors tell us it is okay to be a single person — in fact, we may end up having our Kate and Edith, too.

Goldstine, Larner, Zuckerman, & Goldstine. *The Dance-Away Lover*. New York: Ballantine, 1977. People after divorce do a tremendous amount of distancing while they learn to trust.

*Krantzler, Melvin. *Learning to Love Again*. New York: Thomas Y. Crowell Co., 1977. This book explains many of the aspects of learning to love again after divorce. **

Rogers, Carl. *Becoming Partners*. New York: Dell, 1972. Dr. Rogers interviews several couples with different lifestyles.

Shain, Merle. *Some Men Are More Perfect than Others*. New York: Bantam Books, 1973. A book about men, and hence about women, and love, and dreams.

_____. *When Lovers Are Friends*. Philadelphia: J.B. Lippincott, 1978. **

*Viscott, David. *How to Live with Another Person*. New York: Pocket Books, 1974. This book has many good suggestions on how to build more positive relationships.

Self-Disclosure

Jourard, Sidney M. *The Transparent Self*. New York: D. Van Nostrand Co., 1971. The self-disclosing person has better mental health.

*Powell, John. *Why Am I Afraid to Tell You Who I Am?* Illinois: Argus Communications, 1969. A delightful book that will help you learn to risk opening and sharing yourself.

Sexuality

Comfort, Alex. *The Joy of Sex*. New York: Crown Publishers, 1972.

Transactional-Analysis

*Freed, Alvyn. *T.A. for Tots*. Sacramento, Calif.: Jalmar Press, Inc., 1973. A delightful book to help kids of all ages to better understand the basic principles of T.A.

*James & Jongeward. *Born to Win*. Massachusetts: Addison-Wesley, 1971. A combination of Gestalt and T.A. into one of the best books for helping people become winners. **

Phillips & Cordell. *Am I OK?* Illinois: Argus, 1975. A workbook on using T.A. to help you reach "okayness."

**Also available in mass-market paperback editions. See your bookseller.

notes

notes

notes

notes

notes

notes

notes

notes

notes

notes

Resources For Personal Development...